THE
CLASSIC
HORTICULTURIST

THE
CLASSIC
HORTICULTURIST

URSULA BUCHAN

AND
NIGEL COLBORN

COLLINS
PUBLISHERS

AUSTRALIA

COLLINS PUBLISHERS AUSTRALIA

First published in Australasia in 1988 by William Collins Pty Ltd,
55 Clarence Street, Sydney NSW 2000

National Library of Australia
Cataloguing-in-Publication data:

Buchan, Ursula
The classic horticulturist.

Bibliography.
Includes index.
ISBN 0 7322 0018 0.

1. Horticulture — History — Dictionaries.
2. Botany — Dictionaries.
3. Horticulturists — History.
I. Colborn, Nigel.   II.   Title.

635'.09

ART DIRECTOR Moira Clinch
EDITORIAL DIRECTOR Carolyn King

Typeset by QV Typesetting Ltd
Manufactured in Hong Kong by Regent Publishing
Services Ltd
Printed in Hong Kong by South Sea Int'l Press Ltd.

Quarto Publishing plc would like to take this opportunity
to thank Jacky Morley and Andrew Kidd.

CONTENTS

INTRODUCTION

WHENEVER you bite into a sweet, juicy apple, or select a bunch of grapes, or breathe in the perfume of a blowzy pink rose on a summer evening, do you ever wonder how it is that we are lucky enough to be able to enjoy such pleasures? The enormous wealth of flowers, fruits, herbs and other useful plants that we have inherited is the result not just of natural evolution but of thousands of years of selection, collection and improvement of an almost infinite number of wild plants.

For example, although we might pay a ludicrous price for a bottle of vintage claret, all the currency of the world could not buy the thousands of years of development of the grape — from the time of our neolithic ancestors, who began to train wild vines over posts, through the ancient Persians, Egyptians, Greeks and Romans, the medieval monks ... and so on through history until finally we have the present diversity of vines grown all over the world.

Horticulture — the art and science of gardening — was the first step towards civilization. When our stone-age forebears began to grow their food plants near to their homes, instead of merely gathering nuts and berries from the wild, the resulting abundance gave them more time for other activities — such as thinking. It must be reasonably safe to assume that they gathered seeds or plants from wild stocks, so it follows that they would have selected the best examples. In fact, the art of improving plant varieties must have begun some 10,000 years before the science of genetics emerged. Food production must have been the first objective, but it is possible that certain plants were valued for their supposed magical properties. Later, the healing arts depended on specific plants for herbal remedies and, as civilizations evolved, people began to enhance their places of recreation with plants. Remains of tools have been found in the Tigris valley suggesting that people may have been gardening as early as 5000BC.

Through the ages there have been certain people who, because of their particular abilities, have had considerable influence on the development of horticulture. Some were great plant collectors, others pioneered technical advances, and yet others developed artistry in the garden. To tell the stories of some of these classic horticulturists and their achievements is to tell the story of horticulture itself.

THE HORTICULTURISTS

HORTICULTURE was being practised long before the Hanging Gardens of Babylon were built in about 600BC. The Assyrians collected plants for their temple gardens and there are detailed records of ancient Egyptians growing figs, pomegranates and grapes. The lush silts of the Nile valley, refertilized every year by the river's winter floods, must have provided rich harvests. Queen Hatshepsut was introducing incense trees into her new temple garden between 1500 and 1485BC, and, during the reign of Rameses III (1198-1167BC), trees and shrubs were grown in decorated containers. Egyptian gardens had a line and formality that undoubtedly influenced the Romans, and were in due course to be adopted by the Italians. Today, most good gardens have a great deal in common with those found at the source of Western civilization several thousand years ago.

On the other side of the world the Chinese, during the Ch'in and Han dynasties, were developing the art of landscaping. Their approach seems to have been naturalistic — they enhanced natural scenery with artificial mountains, rock gardens and pools. No doubt shrubs such as the Buddleia (see pages 72-3) were enjoyed both in gardens and in the wild. The idea was to create an area for quiet meditation. The poet Hsieh Ling-Yin (about AD410) wrote[1]:

I have banished all worldly care from my garden, ... I have planted roses in front of the windows, but beyond them appear the hills.

A GREEK HERBAL

Some of the earliest detailed works on horticulture appear in Greek and Roman literature. Dioscorides[2] (*fl.* 1st century) was a Greek practising herbal medicine at about the time that *The Acts of the Apostles* was being written. He was born in Cilicia, and had served in the Emperor Nero's army. He wrote a book about pharmacology, *De Materia Medica*, that was to be used for the next 1500 years. He described the medicinal properties of 600 plants, as well as a large number of animal products which, he claimed, had medicinal value. We know little else about him but, thanks to a horticultural scholar called John Goodyer, Dioscorides' herbal was translated into English in 1655. Goodyer wrote out all 4,540 quarto pages, but the manuscript remained unpublished until the 20th century.[2]

Parts of the work are hard to believe and many of the illustrations are so botched that they bear little resemblance to the original plants — it is likely that they were copied from earlier copies, rather than drawn from life. It must be remembered, too, that our picture of Dioscorides is seen through the eyes of a 17th-

A painting from the Egyptian tomb of Nebamon, dating from c.1400BC. Here we see not only fruit trees in cultivation but also the use of water.

century Hampshire gardener — albeit a well educated one — whose concepts of botany and medicine were quite different from ours. There is a lot of folklore and many of the remedies are fanciful, to say the least. For example:

The stones [? testicles] of hippopotamus, dried and ground up small is drank in wine against the bitings of serpents.

And, on the properties of *Cyclamen*:

They say that if a woman great with childe doe goe over ye roote, that she doth make abortion, and being tied round her it doth hasten the birth.

A painting from the Egyptian tomb of Nebamon, dating from c.1400BC. Here we see not only fruit trees in cultivation but also the use of water.

But there is a wealth of useful information too. He describes how to preserve orris root (*Iris florentina*) and discusses its virtues. He recommends the North African form as being the best and says of the rhizomes: "When they grow old they will be worm-eaten, yet then they smell the sweeter."

When it comes to naming plants, anyone with the merest smattering of botanical knowledge will wince at his classification. Plants were grouped according to their medicinal affinity.

White bryony is placed with the botanically unrelated *Cyclamen* because both have the same pharmaceutical properties. He has the goodness to provide all the known names (around the Middle East at any rate) for each plant. He lists 13 for *Cyclamen hederifolium* — a good example of why a single, internationally recognized name for each plant is such a necessity today.

Dioscorides also seems to have set the trend whereby illustrations show the whole plant, complete with roots, flowers and fruits, on the same page. Although at times this inhibits accurate representation, it does make for economy of space and enables the relevant part of the plant to be shown.

PLEASURE GARDENS OF ROME

Information about Roman gardens can be found in the works of Pliny the Elder (AD23-79)

Roman wall painting from the House of Livia; an early use of *trompe-l'oeil*.

and his nephew Pliny the Younger (AD62-c.114). They were hardly horticulturists — indeed, it is most unlikely that they ever so much as lifted a hoe — but their copious literary output reveals much.

The elder Pliny (Gaius Plinius Secundus) was a top civil servant for the Emperor Vespasian, with whom he was on friendly terms. In spite of a heavy workload, he managed to write a phenomenal number of books. His *Natural History* runs to 37 "volumes", and is a kind of *Life on Earth* without the benefit of scientific observation or colour television! Much of the information is hopelessly wide of the mark, based as it is on stories from unreliable sources. There are reports, for example, of peculiar men *(Sciapodes)* who had such enormous feet that they used them as sunshades, of cherries grafted onto willows, of unicorns, of winged horses, and so on. But there is also some sound material. He describes how a *topiarius* (not exactly someone to do the topiary, but a man employed to train creepers over statues and to keep growth in the gardens tidy) could dwarf planes and conifers with a technique similar to *Bonsai.*[1]

Pliny the Younger (Gaius Plinius Caecilius Secundus) had a lot to say about the plants and gardens of his day. He describes the use of box and rosemary for hedges, trees such as mulberry and fig, and sweet violets — frequently used for underplanting because of their scent. There are details of topiary work (hedges shaped into animals), cypress walks, statues and fountains. Clearly, Roman gardening had much in common with the modern art, and many Roman plants are enjoyed to this day.[3]

THE
MIDDLE AGES

WE know little about what kind of horticulture was being practised in Europe between the decline of the Roman Empire and the Renaissance because records are scarce. The vision one has of that period is of warmongering gentry with private armies slogging out land disputes, while starving peasants squatted in wattle huts, terrified that yet another Viking gang might pop over the North Sea for a bit more rape and pillage. This is an absurdly exaggerated picture, but there was obviously little time for the niceties of artistic plantsmanship.

We do know, however, that after William the Conqueror's invasion of Britain in 1066, the development of new monasteries helped to preserve some of the species the Romans left behind. Plants like Paeonies, Opium poppies and Christmas roses *(Helleborus niger)* (see page 102) which are commonplace today, were grown as medicinal herbs. The 12th-century writer Alexander Neckham (1157-1217) describes such monastic gardening in his *De Naturis Rerum*, although whether he gleaned from practical observation or lifted from earlier literature is not clear. Throughout the next few centuries, records exist of vineyards, of vegetable gardens growing such plants as leeks, carrots and garlic and of fruit orchards. However, it is difficult to find much detailed and reliable information.

By the 15th century, horticulture was making progress again. Between 1400 and 1440, the aptly named Mayster Ion Gardener wrote a treatise called *The Feate of Gardening*. Very little is known about Gardener himself, but it is clear from his work that he had good, working knowledge and was an original

An illustration of a medieval garden from the 15th-century *La Roman de la Rose*, showing peas, irises and double roses.

The right wing of the Wilton Diptych,
c.1395. Campion, liverwort, double roses
and violets are shown.

thinker. Other writers of the time were merely regurgitating the theories of ancient authorities like Pliny the Elder, who had himself written largely from hearsay.[3]

Ion Gardener's text, by contrast, is highly practical and concerns itself solely with the culture of plants for utility. Novel techniques like the grafting of pear trees onto hawthorn are covered — it is interesting to see that clay and hazel bark were used instead of wax and raffia.[3, 4] Instructions on when to sow various seeds are given, and there is a good deal about parsley — an important herb and root vegetable. Gardener knew all about the value of using manure, and describes how to build up soil fertility for growing saffron — a precious medieval commodity, since it took 4,000 crocus flowers to make an ounce.[3] The "Saferowne," he said, must be planted "only in beddys y-made wel with dyng."[4]

Of the 97 plants described in *The Feate of Gardening*, 26 had been introduced from outside Britain. No doubt there were other exotics being grown in monastery gardens and in the great households, but the large-scale collecting of plants had yet to begin.

Although it deals with utilitarian horticulture, Gardener's book mentions both roses and Madonna lilies, *(Lilium candidum)* (see page 110). These two plants both had medicinal uses but it is hard not to believe that, in an age when flowers were beginning to appear in paintings, at least *some* plants were being grown purely for decoration.

THE RENAISSANCE

BY the time Gardener was making his record of horticultural practices, at the beginning of the 15th century, the arts were undergoing something of a rebirth. Up to 1400, records of gardening and botany are scanty and unreliable. The Norman monks must certainly have brought their skills to England: they have been credited with introducing pinks, wallflowers and other plants grown for medicine. We can tell from paintings like the Wilton Diptych (*c.*1395) that certain garden flowers were in cultivation. There are double roses, violets and irises at the Virgin Mary's feet. European wildflowers — Sea catchfly and Liverwort (*Silene vulgaris* and *Hepatica*) — are also shown, and were certainly being grown in the monastery gardens. Although their primary use was probably medicinal, their decorative properties must have been appreciated for them to have been used in such an artistic context.

By the middle of the century, science, painting and music were developing in Europe as never before, but in England the Wars of the Roses were to drag on for another 30 years. However, with the Tudors, innovation became widespread. Sir Thomas More wrote *Utopia* (1516), in which gardens figure as places with attractive flowers and well tended fruit (More had fine gardens laid out for himself at Chelsea), and Cardinal Wolsey built Hampton Court.

THE FIRST BOTANIC GARDENS

In Italy, at this time the epicentre of the Renaissance, gardening was progressing at a greater pace than anywhere else in Christendom. One result of the reborn interest in science was the birth of the botanic garden, the idea springing from the renewed interest in ancient literature: the first botanic gardens in the world were in Pisa and Padua.[1] Elsewhere, plant collecting was to become fashionable, particularly among royalty.

It was into this period of growing interest in new plants that Jules Charles L'Ecluse (Clusius) was born. Clusius was a great botanist and plant collector. With his sound technical education, he was able to observe and record botanical details with unprecedented accuracy. We tend to associate him with tulips — one thinks of the graceful pink and white *Tulipa clusiana* (see page 150) — but he discovered and collected hundreds of different plant species. His description of "Rosa Mundi" (*R. gallica* 'versicolor') — a plant widely grown and gaining popularity among Australasian rose lovers — is the first recorded.

His life was hard and he did not enjoy especially good health.[3] His family were Protestants, then in the minority, so it is likely that they suffered for their religious beliefs. He was well read and widely travelled.

From 1565, he spent a year or so plant hunting in Spain and Portugal. This was interesting for him not just because he could study the native plants but also because the Spanish and Portuguese were at the time bringing exotic plants home from the New World. It is possible that potatoes were already being grown in Spain as early as 1565, a couple of decades before Raleigh grew them in England, and Clusius may have observed them there — although he does not refer to them until much later, when he recalls in his *Rariorum Plantarum Historia* (1601) that he had the plant in 1588.[3]

On his visit to Britain (1571) he read Spanish physician Nicholas Monardes' book about American plants, *Joyfull Newes from the New Found Worlde*, and translated it into Latin (the *lingua franca* of 16th-century scholars) for use in Europe. (Frampton's English translation was not published until 1596.)

In 1573 he laid out a physic garden for Emperor Maximilian II of Austria at Vienna. He spent three years there studying the flora of Austria and Hungary, writing up all his findings in *Historia stirpium per Pannonium*, which was published in 1583. From Austria he moved to Frankfurt where in 1592 he was crippled by a serious fall. In spite of his failing health, he was persuaded by an ardent admirer, Johan van Hoghelande, to accept the post of Director of the Leyden Botanic Garden (part of Leyden University). In this appointment, at

---

JULES CHARLES L'ECLUSE (CLUSIUS)

Father of the Dutch Bulb Industry

—1526—
Born in Arras (then Flemish); later studied law and medicine at Wittenberg and Montpellier

—1565—
Trip to Spain: 200 species recorded

—1566—
Translated d'Orta's Indian Plants

—1571—
Visited England

—1573—
Laid out physic garden for Habsburgs. Studied flora of Austria—Hungary for three years

—1581—
Revisited England. Met Drake

—1587—
Dutch school of gardening formed

—1592—
Serious fall disables him

—1601—
Published Rariorum Plantarum Historia

—1609—
Became Director of Leyden (Hortus Botanicus Lugduni—Batavorum). Died

---

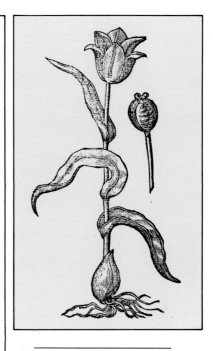

Tulipa clusiana, named after Clusius. This Asian species has been cultivated in Europe for centuries.

---

the end of his life, he introduced some of the first tulips, irises and crocuses. It is thought by some that these became the basis for the development of commercial bulb-production in Holland.

REBIRTH OF THE ROMAN GARDEN

While the botanists were busy collecting and classifying, the Netherlanders were improving cultivational techniques. When the Flemish weavers began to migrate to East Anglia, they brought many of their gardening skills with them. In England, the rich and powerful were having elegant gardens laid out around their houses. The link with ancient Rome was strong,

The frontispiece from Gerard's *Herball*, as originally printed in 1597.

JOHN GERARD

Genius or Plagiarist?

—1545—
Born at Nantwich, Cheshire; later educated at Willaston, near Nantwich

—1577—
Becomes superintendent of Burleigh's gardens in London and Hertfordshire

—1595—
Elected assistant to Barber—Surgeons' Company

—1596—
Published Catalogus arborum fruticum

—1597—
Appointed Junior Warden, Barber—Surgeons' Company and (December) published his Herball, or Generall Historie of Plantes

—1608—
Appointed Master of Barber—Surgeons' Company

—1611—
Died and was buried at St Andrew's, Holborn, London

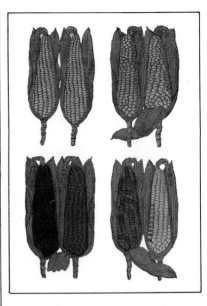

Maize (Indian corn), as illustrated in Gerard's *Herball*.

thanks to the Italian renaissance of classical styles. Gardens were formal and highly geometrical, with clipped hedges. Henry VIII had an artificial mound made at Hampton Court which was planted up with trees and shrubs.

In Elizabeth I's reign the knot garden developed. This consisted of a small area of convoluted hedgery with paths or beds in between. Hedging material was usually box or rosemary, and the beds were filled with coloured gravels or with flowering plants. Knot gardens were not very large — certainly not as large as the impressive French-style parterres.

Small gardens, although they probably contained some plants for beauty, were mainly functional. Thomas Tusser (1515-1580) wrote

Five Hundreth Pointes of Good Husbandrie (1573) which, in verse, describes how the house-wife was landed with all the gardening chores:

> *In Marche and in Aprill,*
> *from morning to night:*
> *in sowing and setting,*
> *good huswives delight,*
> *To have in their garden or*
> *some other plot:*
> *to trim up their house, and*
> *to furnish their pot*
> *Have millons* [*melons*] *at*
> *Michaelmas, parsneps in Lent:*
> *in June, buttred beans,*
> *saveth fish to be spent*
> *With these and good*
> *pottage inough having than:*
> *thou winnest the heart of*
> *thy laboring man.*

SURGEON GARDENERS

The Elizabethans' interest in herbs of all kinds was being stimulated by a succession of new discoveries, particularly from the New World. Surgeons of the day were keen to investigate the pharmaceutical properties of many of the new plants.

A prominent member of the Barber-Surgeons' Company was one John Gerard. Over the years, Gerard has come in for more than his fair share of lambast. Criticism of his *Herball* is well justified on many counts, but it does contain some original work and is an important example of Elizabethan botanical literature. His personality and humour radiate from the text.

Like his rather more famous contemporary, Shakespeare, Gerard came from fairly humble origins. Little is known about his early life, but it is likely that he travelled, probably as a ship's surgeon, before settling down to a London-based career. He married and, presumably, his wife helped him with his work — portions of the *Herball* are "mainly for women".[3] His reputation as a plantsman was well established by the time he was in his early thirties, and he was made superintendent of Lord Burleigh's gardens in London and at Theobalds, Hertfordshire. His own London garden held a collection of more than 1000 varieties, including rarities like double-flowered peach and white thyme.[8] He published details of this collection in *Catalogus arborum fruticum*, which was the first comprehensive catalogue of a private garden ever printed.

His first appointment as an officer in the Company of Barber-Surgeons came when he was 52. (He was steadily promoted until he became Master a few years before his death.) The *Herball* was published in the same year, 1597. The first edition, in spite of being a runaway bestseller, was riddled with mistakes. Some exotics were marked down as British natives and, worse, Gerard had stolen most of the original work from a Belgian botanist called Rembert Dodoens, failing to acknowledge his source. To illustrate the *Herball*, his publisher, John Norton, acquired a job lot of woodcuts from Frankfurt, which in several cases he matched to the wrong text.[1,3] Having cobbled together the miscellany, Gerard added some of his own material and, to secure a stamp of quality and approval, dedicated the book to his patron, Lord Burleigh. The *Herball*'s popularity has remained undiminished for centuries.

One of its most interesting original illustrations is the portrait of Gerard himself. He is depicted holding a potato plant bearing flowers and fruit — the earliest known British picture of a potato. Love Apples (tomatoes) are described too. Early varieties were yellow, hence the Italian *pomadoro*. He says they should be

> sown in a bed of hot horse dung after the maner of muske melons and such like cold fruits.

Gerard's descriptions are concise and clear. Any remarks venturing an opinion are to the point. Of Sweet Williams (*Dianthus barbatus*) (see page 88), for instance, he says:

> These plants are kept and maintained in gardens more to please the eye, than either the nose or belly.

Although historians and botanists accuse Gerard of roguery, few condemn him outright. The *Herball* contains much of merit and its popularity cannot be denied. In the 16th century, copying other people's work was common practice. After all, at the same time, Shakespeare was penning *Julius Caesar* just around the corner from the Barber-Surgeons' Hall. The Bard's material was lifted from Plutarch, without acknowledgement, so who was the worse plagiarist?

THE
17TH CENTURY

*B*Y the time of Elizabeth I's death, the art of gardening in Europe was well developed. Several of her political counsellors, especially the Cecil family, had built grand homes for themselves and were keen to lay out new areas with flowers and fruit as well as to develop parkland. Knot gardens were incorporated into grand terraces which might be lined with walls and stairs or walks of clipped trees. Fountains and waterworks were becoming popular. At Hatfield House these were designed by Chaundler and engineered by a Dutchman — Sturtevant.[3] The essay *Of Gardens* (1625) by Francis Bacon (1561-1626) demonstrates how highly regarded good gardens were becoming in that century:

> *It is the purest of human pleasures; it is the greatest refreshment to the spirits of man; without which buildings and palaces are but gross handyworks.*

On a smaller scale, more people than ever were beginning to indulge in horticulture. Farmers were building larger houses and developing gardens that would provide a more interesting variety of fruit and vegetables. Better textbooks were needed, for the writings of Gerard and Thomas Tusser were becoming dated. Various authors produced helpful volumes, but the major work of the age was written by John Parkinson.

EDEN REVISITED

Parkinson combined three important qualities to create his masterpiece on English gardening, *Paradisi in Sole Paradisus Terrestris*. First, his education and training: as an apothecary he would have developed a detailed knowledge of all the plants used in his day. Second, he was an expert practical gardener who developed his own garden at Longacre and shared his expertise with contemporary botanists like John Tradescant the Elder. Third, he had, beyond scientific knowledge, a profound love and understanding of plants. These qualities, coupled with a talent for fluent and accurate writing, enabled him to produce a book which is both erudite and entertaining to read.

The title is Latin for "A park in the sun — an earthly paradise", a pun on his own name: The frontispiece alone could keep a keen plant historian amused for hours, with all the exotic plants of a 17th-century Eden — including pineapple and prickly pear — in the main body and the disclaimer (in French) at the bottom of the page:

> *Whoever wishes to compare art with nature and our parks with Eden, indiscreetly measures the stride of an elephant by the stride of the mite and the flight of the eagle with that of the gnat.*

The frontispiece from Parkinson's *Paradisi in Sole Paradisus Terrestris*, showing a 17th-century Eden.

JOHN PARKINSON

An Earthly Paradise

—1567—
Born in Nottinghamshire[5]

—Before 1625—
Became apothecary to James I

—1629—
Published Paradisi in Sole Paradisus Terrestris*; became Royal Botanist to Charles I*

—1640—
Published Theatrum Botanicum

—1650—
Died and was buried at St Martins-in-the-Fields, London

A page from Parkinson's *Paradisi in Sole Paradisus Terrestris* showing members of the family Boraginaceae.

There are nine chapters on practical gardening. The size and design of knot gardens is covered in some depth and there are some sound details about materials for their hedging. Cotton lavender, he says, will "perish in some places, especially if you doe not strike or put off the snow, before the sunne lying upon it dissolve it". There is plenty of good advice on siting a new garden, all of it readable and as topical now as it was 350 years ago.

The book goes on to describe a vast range of flowers, fruits and vegetables. The superb illustrations, by the father-and-son team of Christoph and Christoph Switzer, depict many of the var- ieties in fine detail. There are double daffodils, 49 kinds of carnation and double pink, several species of iris ('Fleur de luce'), crown imperials, and so on. Further sections deal with vegetables and fruit, some of whose names are too delightful not to repeat: "The Towne Crab", "The Crowes Egge Apple" and the "Paradise Apple". In the fruit section there is a little eulogy on the benefits of (? fermented) apple juice:

The juice of apples ... is of very good use in melancholicke diseases, helping to procure mirth, and to expell heaviness.

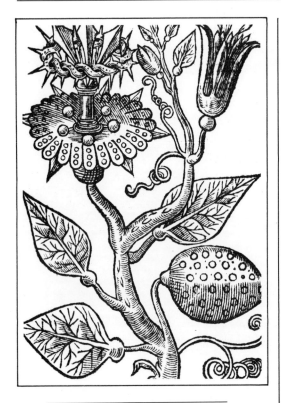

From Parkinson's *Paradisi in Sole Paradisus Terrestris*, an illustration depicting the Jesuits' idea of the Passion flower (*Passiflora*).

In 1640 Parkinson published a complete herbal entitled *Theatrum Botanicum*. Most of the material for this book — unlike *Paradisi*, which was based on his own observations — came from the work of a famous French physician and gardener, Matthias de l'Obel (after whom Lobelias are named).

As a plantsman, Parkinson was much respected and his contribution to gardening in the 17th century is incalculable. However, although he was a great chronicler and cohesive writer, many of the plants he described were collected by others, particularly the Tradescants. He demonstrated how exotic flowers could be used, but it took the obsessive collecting mania of the Tradescant family to help to enrich the world's heritage of garden plants.

STOCKING THE ARK

The lives of the two John Tradescants, father and son, ran from the glorious days of Queen Elizabeth through to the first couple of years of the Interregnum under Oliver Cromwell. Politically, the first two Stuart kings were not a great success but, despite the grim historical events of the era, science and the arts enjoyed tremendous patronage under them. The age began with Shakespeare's last and finest dramas, and went on to produce Inigo Jones, Van Dyck and Rubens. Royal interest in botany, after a strong beginning in Tudor times, was gathering momentum. Ocean transport was becoming safer and the quest was on for new fruits, flowers and vegetables.

John Tradescant the Elder was the son of a Suffolk yeoman who had moved to London.[9, 10] He did not marry until he was 37 and his son was born a year later in 1608.

His first recorded job was with Lord Salisbury, whose gardens were in London and at Hatfield House, some miles north. Hatfield was being revamped, and Tradescant was sent to find new trees for the avenues, fruits and vegetables for the orchards, and flowers for the "pleasure gardens". He introduced new grapevines, White mulberry — in the hope of starting silk production in England — and a number of new roses from France. By 1614 he had left Hatfield and moved to Kent, where he worked as gardener to Sir Edward Wotton.

A few years later, sponsored by Salisbury, he joined Sir Dudley Digges on what turned out to be a most fruitful expedition to Russia. Among many new introductions he brought back seeds of the first larch trees to be grown in Britain. Lord Salisbury had anticipated the expensive nature of the purchasing visit and had made special arrangements with the Treasury to provide bills of exchange, backed by his personal guarantee; these bills served as a kind of traveller's cheque. It is as well that

Tradescant was well financed for, by today's values, his purchases in Russia topped £25,000.

An obsessive nature, acute powers of observation and an indefatigable spirit — as with so many great horticulturists — spurred Tradescant Senior to greater achievements than those of any ordinary gardener. Descriptions of his travels, some of which are on record in his diaries, throw considerable light on his character.[9] It seems he was a great one for taking charge. On the voyage to Russia he nursed the seasick Digges. He observed whales, he caught migrating birds:

> *There were many small birds cam abord the shipe ... I have thre of their skins which were caught by myself.*

One remark suggests — and how unfair of Fate to such a great plantsman if the suggestion is true — that he lacked a sense of smell. He describes a patch of roses:

> *... much like our sinoment [cinnamon] rose; and those that have sense of smelling say they be marvellous sweete.*

He was a great improver, always looking out for better varieties and strains. He brought blackcurrants back from Eastern Europe because they were better flavoured than any in England at the time. The strawberries he left behind. They were

> *nothing differing from ours, but only les, which mad me that I did not so muche seek after them.*

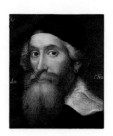

THE TRADESCANTS
Royal Plant Collectors

JOHN TRADESCANT THE ELDER

—1570—
Born in Suffolk

—1607—
Married at Meopham, Kent; subsequently worked for the Cecil family in London and Hatfield

—1614—
Worked for Sir Edward Wotton in Kent

—1618—
First major plant-collecting trip (to Russia)

—1623—
Took over Duke of Buckingham's garden at Newhall, Essex; made Keeper of Royal Gardens at Oatlands

—1626—
Moved to Lambeth

—1637—
Made Keeper of Oxford Botanic Garden, but too ill to take up the appointment

—1638—
Died

The gardens at Hatfield House, more than three centuries after John Tradescant the Elder helped to develop them.

After supervising the Duke of Buckingham's garden in Essex, Tradescant took a house at Lambeth which, because of the huge collection he had developed, became known as The Ark.

PLANTS FROM THE NEW WORLD

By the time John Tradescant the Elder had accepted the job of running the Duke of Buckingham's garden, his talented son, John Tradescant the Younger, was ready to leave King's School, Canterbury, and start an equally successful career in horticulture. No doubt the young enthusiast received the best training possible from his father. When the latter died in 1638, John the Younger succeeded him as Keeper of His Majesty's (Charles I's) Gardens at Oatlands.

The most important events of his career were his three trips to North America between 1637 and 1654. He was responsible for providing us with so many species which today are commonplace that it is hard for us to imagine what life was like without them.

The collection of plants and other artefacts at The Ark had become a famous attraction and, after his father's death, John the Younger set about drawing up a catalogue. This he published in 1654, making it the first catalogue of a private museum ever to be printed.

He had intended to leave the collection to the Crown on his death, but a crafty solicitor, Elias Ashmole, claiming friendship, managed to acquire it for himself. Ashmole bequeathed it to Oxford University, without due acknowledgement to the Tradescant family, where it became the basis of the Ashmolean Museum.[9, 10] Today, the importance of the Tradescants' posthumous contribution to the Ashmolean is at last recognized and acknowledged.

The plants discovered and introduced by the Tradescants are far too numerous to list, but a few examples will serve to show what a huge contribution the two men made. Parkinson mentions some of them in his *Paradisi in Sole Parad-*

JOHN TRADESCANT THE YOUNGER

—1608—
Born at Meopham, Kent

—1623—
Started education at King's School, Canterbury

—1627—
Married Jane Hurte, who died in 1635

—1634—
Made Freeman of Gardeners' Company

—1638—
Appointed Keeper of Royal Gardens at Oatlands, Weybridge

—1638—
Married Hester Pooks

—1637, 1642, 1654—
Plant collecting trips to Virginia

—1654—
Published Musaeum Tradescantianum

—1662—
Died

isus Terrestris. There are pictures of double daffodils such as "Tradescant's Great Rose Daffodil", double martagons, double *Hepatica* and others. London plant trees (see page 128) were also bred from a Tradescant introduction; *Cotinus cogyggria* (Smoke bush, lilac), *Amelanchier ovalis* and *Smilacina racemosa* were theirs. They grew runner beans — as ornamentals, not realizing the food value of the green pods — as well as *Tradescantia* and *Juglans cinerea* (Butternut).

They introduced many new, improved varieties of fruit. Grapevines were brought to Hatfield House together with two new kinds of cherry: 'Archduke's' and 'Biggandre'. During his first visit to Paris Tradescant Senior developed a close relationship with Vespasien Robin, son of Jean Robin, gardener to Louis XIII of France — a friendship which resulted in many valuable plant introductions for Lord Salisbury.[9]

Few families have contributed as much to gardening as the Tradescants. The epitaph on the family tombstone in the graveyard of St. Mary's Church in Lambeth, London, sums up the extent of their explorative natures.

> *Know, stranger, ere thou pass, beneath this stone*
> *Lye John Tradescant, grandsire, father, son,*
> *The last dy'd in his spring, the other two*
> *Liv'd till they had travell'd Orb and Nature through.*

THE RESTORATION

With the end of Cromwell and the restoration of Charles II, the "Merry Monarch", society began to open up. The trend set by the king of going horse-racing, frequenting the theatre and leading a more permissive life than had been acceptable a generation before, was followed by his nobility. It is easy to forget that during this frivolous time Charles also founded the Royal Society to foster science; over 300 years later it is still going strong.

In Restoration gardens French influence ruled — as it was to do for a century. This was the age of the Sun King — Louis XIV — and such creations as Versailles. The biggest single name in French garden design was that of André Le Nôtre (1613-1700). He took the Renaissance designs (themselves inspired by Roman models) and broadened them into huge parterres, symmetrical lines of trees and complicated tapestry bedding. It could be said that the principal difference between English and French gardening at the time was that, while the French subdued nature, the English tried to enhance it. The records of three 17th-century Englishmen — Hanmer, Evelyn and Rea — tell us a great deal about the English interpretation of gardening fashion.

Sir Thomas Hanmer began to write about his garden during the English Civil War, finishing his *Garden Book* in 1659 (although it was not to be published until 1933). The gardens of large houses in the early 17th century were usually laid out in the French style, with formal parterres — knot gardens carried to extremes — consisting of embroidered patterns made with gravels, low hedges and little beds. The hedges were grown into arabesques and curliques so that the overall impression was of a huge patterned carpet.

By the time Charles II came to the throne, the style was changing. Although French influence, as noted, was to dominate garden design

Tradescantia virginiana, one of the countless plants collected by John Tradescant the Younger during his three trips to North America.

for some time to come, the growing interest in plants for their own sake was beginning to necessitate a change in the principles. It is impossible to grow a miscellany of interesting plants in a parterre without ruining it, so it became necessary to provide areas where the special needs of the new style of gardening could be catered for.

The passion for "greens" was getting under way at this time. Greens were evergreen plants in large containers which could be stood out in summer but which were brought indoors for winter — hence the name "greenhouses". Oranges were used for this purpose, their aromatic evergreen foliage being prized for its

Agapanthus umbellatus from
an 1800 issue of *Curtis'*
Botanical Magazine.

SIR THOMAS HANMER

A Garden in Wales

—1612—
Born in Welsh borders

—1646—
Retired to garden in
Flintshire to avoid Civil
War

—1659—
Finished his Garden
Book *(not published*
until 1933)

—1679—
Died

brightness. Various kinds of holly and laurel were used, as well as bay, oleander and *Viburnum tinus* (see page 152).

Hanmer's favourite plants were bulbs, particularly tulips. He called them

> *the Queen of bulbous plants, whose flower is beautiful in its figure, and most rich and admirable in colour, and the wonderful variety of markings.*

He describes nerines too, calling them "narcissus of Japan" — odd, because they are South African natives. (Most gardeners were as ignorant of the origins of exotic plants then as they are today.)

Hanmer writes up details of his fruit collection in Flintshire, particularly of his pears and grapes, of which a wide variety was then available. He also gives details of the plants he purchased, and it is staggering to see how expensive nursery stock then was: clearly, plant buying was not for the masses. He mentions, in 1667, having paid two shillings each for peach trees, three shillings for nectarine trees, and eightpence for Gillyflower (double pink) roots.[3] This writer remembers his mother buying pinks at Romford Market for eightpence each in 1957. Evidently, nurserymen fared rather better during the Restoration.

EVELYN'S DIARIES

Hanmer was a flower and fruit man. The first love of John Evelyn was trees. As a forestry expert he wrote about trees and their uses both as ornaments and as sources of timber. Of all the characters in this brief history, he is the most public. Many know him for his diaries, which describe his milieu, although not half so well as do those of Samuel Pepys. But he was a keen and educated gardener with a particular knowledge of trees. His book *Sylva, or A Discourse of Forest Trees* (1664) was a standard work to be used for another 100 years.[3] He was the first to recommend planting trees for the specific purpose of supplying wood — to the Royal Navy. Strangely enough, despite the soundness of his advice, no government attempted to initiate tree-planting for the Navy until the Napoleonic Wars.

Evelyn was not deeply impressed by the beauty of the parterre. He found straight lines and symmetry less to his taste than natural views. He enjoyed open parkland or woodland with broad, generous rides running through it. These rides, he claimed, enabled one to enjoy the view but, at the same time, there were trees nearby to offer shelter from the weather and to act as cover for game. He was also keen on encouraging songbirds, which were able to nest in the sheltered rides. He said they were "never found in lofty woods where they are exposed to hawks and owls".

In 1664 he published his *Kalendarium Hortense* in which he gives useful details for each month, such as the signs of the Zodiac, times of sunrise, and hours of daylight. There are sections on jobs of the month and notes on which plants are in their prime.

Evelyn was the first writer to describe a heated greenhouse (at the Apothecaries' Garden, Chelsea). In a later publication he describes a design of his own. In an age without fungicides, poorly ventilated greenhouses could soon result in "greens" being wiped out by botrytis and other fungal diseases. Evelyn's patent system was based on heat exchange: the draught of the flue was used to evacuate stale air from the building while, at the same time,

The first nerines in Britain (*N. sarniensis*), were described by Hanmer in his *Garden Book*. Shown here is the similar, but more robust, *N. bowdenii*.

fresh, heated air was drawn in by the resulting negative pressure inside the house.

Evelyn's own garden at Sayes Court in Deptford, London, was well known, and he frequently describes it in his diary. In the hard winter of 1683-84 the Thames froze over and a whole street-system of booths and shops was set up on the ice. In that February he writes:

I went to Says Court ... where I found many of the Greens and rare plants utterly destroyed; The Oranges and Myrtils very sick, the Rosemary and Lawrell dead to all appearance, but the cypress like to endure it out.

An event took place in 1698 which serves well as an object lesson in how to choose one's guests. Evelyn's pride and joy at Sayes Court was his 120m-long holly hedge. When he lent his house to the Czar of Russia — Peter the Great — His Majesty thought it would be fun to vandalize the garden, and he almost managed to wreck the beautiful hedge.[3] Describing the strength and beauty of the holly, Evelyn says: "It mocks at the rudest assaults of weather, beasts, or hedgebreakers."

Evelyn's writings were prolific. He was a well known scholar and society man.

JOHN REA — GENTLEMAN GARDENER

John Rea was a less flamboyant character than Evelyn but his book,

JOHN EVELYN

Diarist

—1620—
Born at Wotton, near Dorking, Surrey

—1638—
Educated at Balliol College, Oxford

—1643—
Visited Europe

—1647—
Married Mary Browne in Paris

—1649—
Published the first of his three dozen books (a translation)

—1660—
After tacitly supporting Royalist cause, was well received by Charles II on his accession

—from 1662—
Served on Royal Commissions on civil matters

—1662—
Elected to Royal Society

—1664—
Published Sylva, or a Discourse of Forest Trees *and* Kalendarium Hortense

—1685—
James II acceded to throne; Evelyn appointed Commissioner of the Privy Seal

—1706—
Died and was buried at Wotton

By the 17th century, tulips were widely grown in Europe. *Tulipa clusiana* was a popular species.

based on his own experiences, provides a delightful portrait of 17th-century English gardening. In fact, very little is known about Rea the man: all we have is the only book he wrote, *Flora, Ceres et Pomona* (1665). He styled himself "Gentleman", was a close friend of Sir Thomas Hanmer, and his book is one of the best gardening works to come out of the Restoration period. He had what must have been a fascinating garden at Kinlet in Worcestershire. That he was a first-rate plantsman is evident from *Flora, Ceres et Pomona*, which is subtitled: *A complete Florilege, fur-*

nished with all requisites belonging to a florist. He dedicated this work to, among others, members of the Hanmer family.

By the latter half of the 17th century, so many new plants had been introduced that Parkinson's *Paradisi in Sole* of 1629 was going out of date. Rea felt that there were too few good gardens about and promoted the idea of gardening quite strongly:

> *Fair houses are more frequent than fine gardens; the first effected by artificers, the latter requiring more skill in their owner.*

He goes into considerable detail about how to lay out a garden, with advice on where to build walls, which bits to have near the house and so on. He suggests that size should be limited, for "large gardens are usually ill-furnished and ill-kept". A nobleman, he suggests, might want about 73m of fruit and 27m of flowers; a private gentleman — someone like himself, presumably — would be able to get by with only 37m of fruit.[3] On the subject of fruit, he discusses how to graft pears onto quince stocks.

His advice about flowers is interesting but not always to modern tastes. The idea of having several different varieties of rose grafted to the same standard stock sounds a little grotesque by today's standards but is no less so than, say, standard fuchsias. He was one of the first to discuss how plants asso-

JOHN REA
Gentleman Gardener

—?—
Born

—1665—
Published Flora, Ceres et Pomona

—1681—
Died

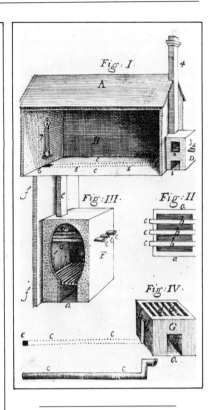

Evelyn's greenhouse allowed stale cool air to be exhausted while fresh warmed air was drawn in.

ciate with each other, and he describes a small bed with paeonies in the centre and dwarf anemones, ranunculi, tulips and irises round the outside. Gertrude Jekyll could have suggested the same combination a couple of hundred years later.

There are some helpful ideas on siting a summerhouse so that it can double as a bulb-sorting and -storing shed in the winter. He describes the service area of the garden in detail — the nursery, storehouses, hotbed and greenhouse. Rea shared Hanmer's love of tulips and their undeniable beauty even moved him to verse:[3]

> *The tulips to delight your eyes,*
> *With glorious garments, rich and new,*
> *Like the rich glutton some are dight*
> *In Tyrian-purple and fine white;*
> *And in bright crimson others shine*
> *Impal'd with white and graydeline*
> *[purple]:*
> *The meanest here you can behold,*
> *Is cloth'd in scarlet, Lac'd with gold.*
> *But then the queen of all delight*
> *Wears graydeline scarlet and white:*
> *So interwov'n and so plac'd,*
> *That all the others are disgrac'd*
> *When she appears and doth impart*
> *Her native beauties shaming art.*

Rea classifies his tulips according to their flowering period — early, middle and late — and describes nearly 200 varieties. He writes about a fair number of daffodils as well as molys *(Allium)*, asphodels, colchicums, gladioli and cyclamen. There are sections on auriculas, with special reference to particular varieties from places like the Oxford Botanic Garden.[3] The 1648 catalogue of the Oxford Botanic Garden contains details of a great number of rare primroses, including a blue one.[3] In the *Pomona* section of his masterpiece, Rea covers many of the types of fruit we enjoy from modern orchards plus several, like *Sorbus* and medlars, which are rarely eaten nowadays. The familiar pear-names 'Chrétien' and 'Beurré' are listed.

Rea's is a book based on his own practical experience. He loved his garden and wrote about what he loved. He said: "It is knowledge that begets affection, and affection increaseth knowledge." He had no time for those who paid merely lip-service to plants. His dismissal of people who fail to recognize the value of a good plant is as apt now as in 1665:

> *I have known many Persons of Fortune pretend much affection to Flowers, but very unwilling to part with anything to purchase them; yet if obtained by begging, or perhaps by stealing, contented to give them entertainment.*

Oxford Botanic Gardens, visited by Linnaeus in 1735. Species of Mullein and Veronica can be seen.

THE 18TH CENTURY

*T*OWARDS the end of the 17th century, the increasing demand for plants presented commercial nurserymen with novel opportunities. The passion for standing hundreds of elegant pots about the place, each one planted with decorative "greens", was at its height. The number of species and varieties in cultivation grew bigger every year but, until this time, most nursery stock was imported, mainly from Holland. By the end of the century, George London had started to direct the first large professional nursery of its kind in England.

London was a self-made man of humble background.[3,4] He was taken as pupil by John Rose, gardener to Charles II, who sent him to France, then the fount of gardening wisdom, to complete his apprenticeship. Around this time he was involved in the setting-up of the Brompton Park Nursery. The French sojourn was followed, in 1685, by a trip to Leyden, Holland, where he got to know a good deal about Dutch horticulture; the knowledge gained on these trips proved invaluable for his own nursery business later. On his return to England from Holland, he was appointed gardener to Bishop Compton, at Fulham, and proved himself to be exceptionally loyal and reliable. He became embroiled in the Glorious Revolution of 1688, when he was called upon by his master — and by Lady Marlborough — to assist in the escape of Princess (later Queen) Anne.

At about this time he teamed up with Henry Wise, and together they worked at a large number of gardens including Chatsworth, Blenheim and Windsor.[4]

By 1688, William and Mary were on the throne. George London was appointed superintendent of the Royal Gardens. In this post he was responsible for Hampton Court where, with Wise, he laid out "a great fountain garden" near Wren's new East Front. The famous maze was also their work; it was originally planted with hornbeam. Interestingly, the first recorded flowering Agapanthus was at this garden.

Hampton Court took up most of the royal budget for parks and gardens in London. In 1702, expenditure on plants and upkeep came to £1,623 out of a total budget of less than £2,000.[3] George London's annual fee for supervising the planting was £200. For a part-time job, this seems a princely sum, compared with a full-time gardener's weekly wage of four shillings, or a foreman's twelve shillings.

London's other great achievement had been, as we have noted, to set up the enormous Brompton Park Nursery at Kensington. The site is occupied today by the Natural History Museum, but in 1681 a consortium, headed by London, started the new business on 40 hectares — an ambitious plot by any standards. Other members of the consortium

The great semicircular garden at
Hampton Court, laid out by London and
Wise during the reign of William and
Mary.

were Moses Cook, John Field and Roger Lookar. All were important gardeners — Lookar, in particular, was gardener to Charles II's wife, Catharine of Braganza. Henry Wise joined the firm in 1689, and its name was changed to "London & Wise".[3]

The name of the nursery's game was "greens". A monumental greenhouse — bigger than the king's own — was built, and production increased rapidly. By the turn of the century the firm employed a score of labourers and held stocks of more than a million plants. By the end of London's life, however, the craze for containerized evergreens was beginning to wane. Within a year of London's death Wise sold up his share of the nursery, and soon afterwards it went into decline.

A DEDICATED PLANTSMAN

While the fashion for "greens" was fading, the urge to collect plant species was still as strong as ever. Botanic and physic gardens existed all over Europe, and new introductions were continuing to pour into cultivation. Breeding, too, was fast developing. The degree of success of any garden depends on the calibre of the people who run it. One British physic garden achieved world fame largely because of the energy of one of its early gardeners.

The story of Philip Miller is linked with the development and success of the Chelsea Physic Garden in London. Towards the end of the 17th century, the Apothecaries' Company had wanted to acquire some land outside London on which to grow their collection of medicinal plants. In 1673 they leased a parcel of riverside ground from Charles Cheyne, very close to where Sir Thomas More's estate had been in Henry VIII's reign. The soil was light and fertile and, once the enclosure had been walled in, they had a sheltered spot in which to grow their exotics. In 1722 Sir

Hans Sloane, himself a keen botanist, purchased all the land and conveyed it to the Apothecaries' Company, subject to certain conditions: the garden was to be properly managed and, for 40 years, 50 new species per year were to be grown in the garden. A dried, mounted specimen of each new plant was to be presented to the Royal Society. This ensured that at least 2,000 new plants would be introduced before 1762.[11] The apothecaries appointed a professional florist as gardener, and in Philip Miller they made a wise choice. He was to work at the Physic Garden for a staggering 48 years.

Miller, a Quaker with Scottish ancestry, was instilled with a deep commitment to hard work. His father had come south to set up a market garden in Kent, and so Miller would have grown up with the florist's art. (Florists were breeders and selectors of specific plants, not flower traders.) His *Gardeners' and Florists' Dictionary* (1724) became the standard reference work for florists for more than a century. His encyclopedic knowledge of plants and his practical background were helpful, but in addition to these qualities, he was lucky enough to be possessed of green fingers. There are scientists alive today who may be spearheading the frontiers of botany, but who need merely to glance at a geranium to have it wither and die. Others, without a scrap of formal training, can tear off bits of plant at the wrong time of year and still have them root in a

GEORGE LONDON

Nurseryman and Landscape Expert

−1640−
Born

−1681−
Partner in Brompton Park Nursery

−1685−
Visited Leyden

−1687−
Joined by Wise; worked with Wise at Chatsworth and elsewhere

−1688−
Glorious Revolution; assisted Princess Anne to escape; appointed superintendent of Royal Gardens for William and Mary

−1700−
Invited to design gardens at Castle Howard

−1713−
Died

The frontispiece to the *Gardener's Kalendar* for 1745, showing Flora welcoming the god of horticulture.

matter of days. Miller had both the training and the "way" with plants.

Hotbed culture — the heat generated by the decomposing material in the bed is supposed to protect the items planted in it — was a Miller speciality. Greenhouses and stove-houses were used for tropical plants, and one of the most celebrated trees in the collection, mentioned earlier by Evelyn, was the Jesuit Bark (quinine). The cedars of Lebanon at Chelsea became quite famous, too. They were not the first to be planted in England — John Watts, one of the early curators, planted them in 1683 — but they were the first in England to produce cones.[3]

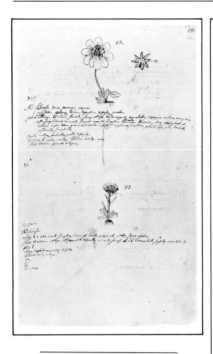

A page from Linnaeus' notebook, illustrating two Scandinavian natives, *Dryas* and *Erigeron*.

PHILIP MILLER

The Chelsea Physic Garden

—1691—
Born

—1722—
Appointed gardener, Apothecaries' Garden, Chelsea (Chelsea Physic Garden)

—1724—
Published Gardeners' and Florists' Dictionary

—1736—
Linnaeus visited Chelsea Physic Garden

—1771—
Died

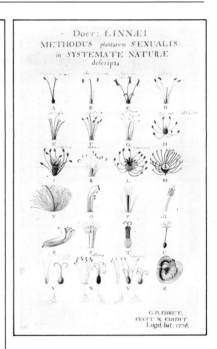

One of Linnaeus' illustrations of the morphology of flowering plants, showing the stamens and pistils of various species.

Miller received Linnaeus at Chelsea in 1736, and the fact that the great man visited at all shows how much the garden, with its extensive collection of rare plants, had grown in international stature since Miller's appointment. Miller, by 16 years the older man, disagreed with Linnaeus' new taxonomic theories until many years later, when he adopted them in revised versions of his *Dictionary.*

Miller, in his declining years, made the mistake of clinging too long to his appointment. The fame of the Chelsea garden became overshadowed by Kew which, under the vigorous management of William Aiton, became the botanist's Mecca. However, to this day the Chelsea Physic Garden remains an important repository of rare plants.

An example of how such places can serve mankind can be seen in the North American cotton story. According to Dr Dawtrey Drewitt,[11] writing in 1922, Miller sent a packet of upland cotton seed to Georgia in 1732. From that single original packet grew the North American cotton industry. A little hard to swallow perhaps, but not impossible.

Towards the end of the 18th century, French influence declined. English love of nature was breaking through the strictures of regimented planting. Parterres were going; broad, sweeping lawns were coming in. By 1760, work at Stourhead had begun, and with it came the fashion of constructing lakes large enough to reflect a topography decorated with trees and shrubs. The second half of the century saw the works of the great landscapers Lancelot "Capability" Brown and Humphry Repton.

THE NAMING OF PLANTS

Botanical science was moving forward rapidly, too. With so many new plants to classify, the world was crying out for someone clever enough to introduce a soundly based taxonomy. Such a man was the Swedish-born Carl von Linné (Carolus Linnaeus).

Before we complain about the awkwardness of Latin names for plants, we should ponder on how things were before an agreed international naming system was developed. With colloquial names confusion reigns. In England, for example, the name "Grannies' Bonnet" refers to: *Aquilegia vulgaris*, *Geum rivale* and *Silene alba*. If you talk to a Japanese botanist about "brandy bottles", you will confuse him, but he is likely to recognize the name *Nuphar lutea*. True, some scientific names seem unnecessarily difficult — who could forgive the boffins for *Paeonia mlokosewitschii?* — but at least they are standard throughout the world.

Botanists had attempted to find a satisfactory way of classifying plants for centuries, but it was Linnaeus who developed a system of naming pretty well everything that lived. He was not only a brilliant botanist but a first-rate doctor of medicine: he ran a successful practice in Stockholm, and developed a new cure for certain venereal diseases.[12]

His passion for plants and flowers began during childhood. His father, a curate at Smaland, had a plantsman's garden at his vicarage. After a year at Lund University, Linnaeus went to Uppsala, where he qualified and where he was offered a lectureship in botany at the

The Chelsea Physic Garden, made famous by Philip Miller. The statue in the centre is of Sir Hans Sloane.

youthful age of 23. In 1735 he travelled to Holland and took another medical degree, at Hardewijk. During this period he went to England to visit the famous Apothecaries' Garden at Chelsea where, as we saw, he met Miller. He went on to the Oxford Botanic[3] Garden but returned to Sweden in 1738.

There followed a period of practising medicine; during this time the University of Uppsala offered him their chair in medicine. His intellectual talents were, by now, phenomenal, and he was able to present lectures in zoology, botany, geology, medicine and hygiene; in addition, he was an accomplished writer and poet! He was appointed Royal Physician and, by 1758, had generated enough wealth to be able to buy a country estate at Hammerby, just outside Uppsala.[12] Recognition came from King Adolphus Frederick of Sweden, who honoured him with the title von Linné.

ural characteristics. There was worldwide agreement that *Species plantarum* and the fifth edition (1754) of *Genera plantarum* together provided the starting point for international nomenclature.

Linnaeus in the costume of a Laplander. His tour of Lapland in 1732 led to a detailed study of the flora.

Linnaeus' most important works were the 1735 *Systema naturae*, the 1737 *Genera plantarum* and the 1753 *Species plantarum*. With the growing numbers of new species being discovered in the 18th century, the world was crying out for a reliable classification system. Linnaeus' plant nomenclature was scientifically based. Everything was grouped into genera and species; every plant had a binomial name. (*Genus*, beginning with a capital letter, and *species*, with a small letter — thus *Bellis perennis*.) Classification was based on the plant's anatomy. He used such parameters as numbers of stamens, numbers of pistils, and whether petals were joined or free, so that botanists could place any plant into a named category based on its nat-

CARL VON LINNÉ (CAROLUS LINNAEUS)

The Principle of Genera and Species

—1707—
Born May 23rd at South Rashult, Sweden

—1730—
Became lecturer in Botany at Uppsala University

—1732—
Visited Lapland

—1735—
Produced Systema naturae

—1737—
Published Flora Lapponica *and* Genera plantarum

—1739—
Married

—1741—
Appointed to the Chair of Medicine at Uppsala University

—1742—
Exchanged his Chair in Medicine for that in Botany

—1753—
Published Species plantarum

—1761—
Ennobled, and granted the title von Linné

—1774—
Suffered serious stroke

—1778—
Died and was buried at Uppsala Cathedral

As well as his work on taxonomy, Linnaeus produced some important reference works on botany. He explored Lapland in 1732 and wrote a detailed flora for that region which was published in 1737 and translated into English in 1811 by J.E. Smith. (Smith was first president of the Linnaean Society — a scientific club which he started with Sir Joseph Banks in 1788, when they managed to purchase Linnaeus' library and herbarium from Sweden.) A Swedish flora was published in 1745, followed by a fauna in 1746.

In 1755 the King of Spain invited Linnaeus to settle in Spain with a large salary. This tempting offer Linnaeus declined, preferring to continue his work in Sweden.

In 1774 he suffered a serious stroke, and from then onwards his health failed. He spent the last four years of his life in a state of semi-consciousness; his death in 1778 came as a release. He was buried in Uppsala Cathedral.

Linnaeus was a very great man with a giant intellect. Of him, King Gustav III of Sweden said:

> *I have lost a man who has done honour to his country as a loyal subject, as well as being renowned throughout the world.*[12]

Gustav III was correct: Linnaeus' impact on botany spread far beyond Sweden's shores. When the English botanist Sir Joseph Banks sailed from Plymouth aboard the *Endeavour* in 1768 as a paying member (the trip cost Banks £10,000, a fortune at the time) on James Cook's first great voyage of discovery into the Pacific he took along his naturalist friend Dr Daniel Solander, Linnaeus' favourite pupil, as his right-hand man.

Cook circumnavigated the world, visiting Tahiti, Brazil, Australia, New Zealand, the East Indies and South Africa, while Banks crammed the small ship with drawings and dried specimens of some 3,000 plant species, of which 1,000 were completely new to science. Among the plants recorded by artist Sydney Parkinson were acacias, banksias, proteas, eucalyptus — Banks was the first person to call them gums — grevilleas and callistemons. The engravings from this voyage have been preserved as Banks' *Florilegium.*

The voyage caused a sensation and made Banks' reputation as a pivotal figure in the scientific establishment. His London house in Soho Square, with its natural history collections and a magnificent library run by Solander, became a mecca for visiting scientists. Banks was elected president of the Royal Society in 1778, exerting immense power over scientific matters from botany to engineering until his death in 1820.

Research was not his forte. His

SIR JOSEPH BANKS
Gentleman Plant
Collector

—1743—
Born February 13th at
Westminster in London

—1766—
Elected fellow of Royal
Society. Collected plants
in Newfoundland

—1768—
Chief botanist on Cook's
voyage to Pacific which
lasted until 1771

—1772—
Visited Iceland

—1778—
President of the Royal
Society

—1805—
Published A Short
Account of the Causes
of the Disease called the
Blight, Mildew and Rust

—1820—
Died June 1820

writing output was insignificant, and he never published a definitive account of his voyage with Cook. Instead he exercised enormous influence as a grand patron, promoting expeditions to Africa, Australia, South America, China and elsewhere. He tirelessly advocated numerous ambitious schemes, including the settlement of New South Wales (advising Arthur Phillip, the first governor, what seeds to take to Botany Bay in 1787, thus playing an early role in the development of Sydney's Botanic Gardens) and the growth of tea in India.

His reign at the Royal Society paralleled the rule of Kew as the major botanic institution in England, sending out dozens of intrepid plant hunters, many recommended by Banks. These peripatetic botanists included such luminaries as Francis Masson, Allan Cunningham, David Nelson, George Caley, William Ker, Peter Good and James Bowie, all of whom made invaluable contributions to our understanding of botany.

The era of Banks' tutelage over the botanic establishment ended with his death, when Kew was superseded by the Royal Horticultural Society. However, plant hunters continued to probe the unknown with many visiting The Antipodes, notably Cunningham, Robert Brown and Ferdinand von Mueller in Australia and Thomas Cheeseman, William Colenso and Sir Leonard Cockayne in New Zealand, throughout the 19th century.

THE
19TH CENTURY

BY 1800 the English style of garden, as typified by places like Stourhead, was beginning to influence the world as strongly as had the French 100 years before. Areas colonized by the British were to inherit their style of gardening. Climate made a difference to the type of plants used, but not to the style. One of the finest examples in the tropics is at Peradeniya, Sri Lanka, started in 1821. Botanic gardens were laid out also in Singapore (1822), Trinidad (1819) and Jamaica (1774). One of the loveliest, not only for its layout with lawns, natural groups of trees and flowering plants, but also for its magnificent position in a quiet harbour cove, is at Sydney, Australia.

BEGINNINGS OF "VILLA" GARDENING

Small gardens, too, were beginning to develop. Changes in the social structure of the civilized world were to mean changes in gardening habits. One of the first visionaries to herald this new age was John Claudius Loudon.

Loudon was born within a few years of the death of Linnaeus. In Europe it was an ominous time: the French Revolution was about to shake the old establishment to its roots, the first convicts were being sent to Botany Bay, and George III was showing signs of lunacy. The Agricultural Revolution was progressing rapidly, soon to be followed by the dawn of modern industry.

Up to the 19th century gardening was either carried on by cottagers — more from necessity than for pleasure — or indulged in on a grand scale by wealthy landowners. By 1800, with changing fortunes, a number of newly successful individuals were building "villas" for themselves. By today's standards these properties would have been considered large — perhaps 4 hectares of grounds and half a dozen principal bedrooms — but they were really small-scale imitations of the large landowners' mansions. A middle class was emerging too, and with it a taste for suburban life and suburban gardening. John Loudon was one of the main innovators in this new mass-gardening age.

An illustration from an 1832 edition of Loudon's *Gardeners' Magazine*, showing an early lawn mower.

He was born in 1783 near Edinburgh, where he went to school until he was 14. His thirst for knowledge of all kinds was prodigious. He was fascinated by scientific subjects, especially chemistry, and he was a capable draughtsman. Because of his love of plants, his father sent him as an apprentice to a local nurseryman, under whom he studied trees and their culture with such intensity that he soon became an authority. During his apprenticeship he taught himself French and Italian. In 1803 he went to London, intending to set himself up as a freelance journalist. He made friends with Sir Joseph Banks, who allowed him access to his private library and who, no doubt, encouraged his advancement. Certainly Banks assisted in Loudon's election into the Linnaean Society in 1806.

In 1813, after Napoleon's retreat from Moscow but before he had been defeated in France and packed off to Elba, Loudon took it into his head to travel to Russia. For a normal person, such a trip would be about as much fun as a sightseeing tour of Warsaw in 1942. But Loudon was tougher than most. The adventures that befell him on the way make better reading than any fiction: he was attacked by Cossacks, left alone in a snowdrift surrounded by howling wolves, and arrested as a spy.[13] In spite of the vicissitudes of the trip — Moscow was a smoking ruin — he managed to visit every famous garden and to make his mark on Russian society. He was elected a member of the

JOHN AND JANE LOUDON

First Steps to Popular Gardening

JOHN CLAUDIUS LOUDON

—1783—
Born April 8th in Lanarkshire; later educated in Edinburgh

—1797—
Apprenticed to a nurseryman; taught himself French, Italian

—1803—
Moved to London

—1806—
Elected to Linnaean Society

—1807—
Right arm amputated

—1813—
Visited Russia

—1822—
Published Encyclopaedia of Gardening

—1826—
Launched The Gardeners' Magazine

—1831—
Designed Birmingham Botanic Garden

—1830—
Married Jane Webb

—1836—
Launched The Suburban Gardener

—1838—
Published Arboretum et Fruticetum Britannicum

—1840—
Visited Europe

—1843—
Died (December 14th)

Imperial Society of Moscow. His impression of Russian nobility was not so favourable. He wrote:

A barbarous people may hang together by a sort of tattered moral principle ... the simple principle of self preservation.

As an excessively hard worker, it is not surprising that Loudon had managed to make himself pretty well off by the time he was 30. By 1812, through writing, farming as a tenant in Middlesex and Oxfordshire, and landscape consultancy, he was worth £15,000.[13] In 1823 he built himself a comfortable house in Porchester Terrace, Bayswater, about a mile from Marble Arch, London. It was typical of the sort of villa that successful men were building for themselves. In its tiny domed conservatory he built up a collection of Camellias. (Conservatories were yet to reach Victorian grandeur as seen today at Kew and at Longwood, Pennsylvania.)

His *Encyclopaedia of Gardening*, published in 1822, was aimed at people who, like himself, were fairly new to gracious living. The *Encyclopaedia* is a "how to" book of roughly 1.1 million words with helpful illustrations and descriptions. First comes a long section about the history of gardening, followed by details of tooling-up for the estate, man-management and plants. It has been compared with Mrs Beeton's *Household Management*, doing for small estate management what she did for housekeeping.

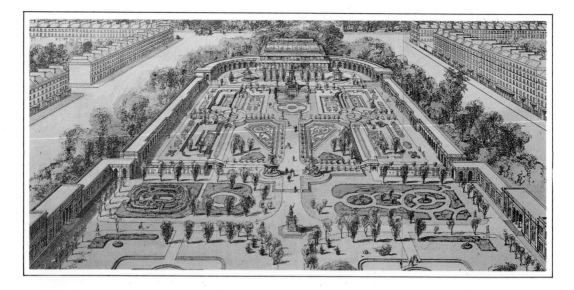

Overwork, carried to Loudon's feverish extremes, did nothing for his health. He suffered from rheumatics, particularly in his right arm. As a result of charlatan treatment, the arm was accidentally broken and amputation was advised. His behaviour at what must have been an excruciating operation was stoical to say the least. One of his draughtsmen was staying with him at the time and recorded the event:

> *After lunch he walked upstairs [for the operation] quite composedly, talking to the doctors on general subjects. When all the ligatures were tied, and everything was complete, he was about to step downstairs, as a matter of course, to go on with his business; and the doctors had great difficulty to prevail upon him to go to bed.*[13]

Rheumatism developed also in the other arm, so that he could move only his third and fourth fingers.

In 1826 he launched one of the first popular gardening magazines: *The Gardener's Magazine.* A couple of years later he came across a new, futuristic novel, *The Mummy! A Tale of the Twenty-Second Century,* by Jane Webb. It con-

The gardens of the Royal Horticultural Society at Kensington. In 1822, the society moved to a larger site at Chiswick.

tained descriptions of 22nd-century mechanical ploughs and milking machines. He was so impressed that he wrote a review in *The Gardener's Magazine* and contrived to meet the author. They met in February 1830 and were married the following September. She became his right hand — almost literally! — taking dictation, helping him direct the gardeners, and fetching and carrying for him with total devotion.

BOTANIST BY MARRIAGE

At the time of her wedding, Jane Loudon said:

> *It is scarcely possible to find any person more completely ignorant of everything to botany and gardening, than I was at the period of my marriage with Mr Loudon ...*

But, like her husband, she had a hungry mind and was a keen worker. She began to attend the lectures of Professor John Lindley at University College, London, and, with expo-

An illustration from Jane Loudon's *Ladies' Flower Garden of Ornamental Perennials* (1844).

JANE WELLS LOUDON née WEBB

—1807—
Born August 19th in Birmingham

—1827—
Published The Mummy!

—1830—
Married John Loudon

—1831—
Went on tour of gardens in the North

—1840—
Published Gardening for Ladies

—1841—
Began to publish Ladies' Companion to the Flower Garden *series of books*

—1843—
Published The Entertaining Naturalist; *continued to publish further garden books until:*

—1852—
My Own Garden, *her last book*

—1858—
Died

sure to her husband's fund of knowledge, picked up a phenomenal amount of information in a very short time. The Loudons became a productive team. As his amanuensis, she helped him to complete his most important book, *Arboretum et Fruticetum Britannicum*, a massive undertaking in eight volumes, published in 1838.

On a trip to Birmingham, a few months after their wedding, the Loudons visited Chatsworth, in Derbyshire, where Joseph Paxton, one day to build the Crystal Palace and receive a knighthood, was head gardener. Although they became friends, Loudon and Paxton were natural opposites. Loudon disliked what Paxton was doing with the gardens at Chatsworth, where flamboyant bedding-out was practised. For Loudon, the beauty of individual plants mattered more than the mass effect, which he found unpleasantly ostentatious. In his own garden in Bayswater he had a rich collection of more than 3,000 species. Every inch of ground was used yet, despite the profusion, the garden was well designed and pleasing to the eye. It seems ironic that, despite Loudon's botanical approach to villa gardening, the Victorians were to abandon plantsmanship and go for jazzy bedding out in its place.

By 1840 Loudon was ill and in debt. He was working neurotically hard, landscaping, designing cemeteries and writing, frequently through the night. This meant that Jane would have to write through the night as well, for it was at his dictation that she worked. She was also producing her own *Gardening for Ladies* (1840) and the *Ladies' Companion* series at this time. A crushing blow came when his major creditor went bankrupt. The wolves closed in on Loudon at a time when he was too ill to do much more than dictate to his wife. They managed to borrow some money from Joseph Strutt of Derby, but Loudon had to assign the copyright of his forthcoming book on Repton to his creditors. At dawn on December 14th, 1843, after an all-night dictating session, he collapsed in his wife's arms and died.

Jane Loudon continued to live at Porchester Terrace until her own death, 15 years later. She had become Britain's leading garden writer, and had published a considerable number of books about natural history and plants.

MODERN TIMES

THE Loudons' love of naturalism in landscapes and gardens, although it went out of fashion for a generation, set the trend for modern "informal" gardening. Although one can still find uncomfortable reminders of the Victorian bedding craze in public parks, corporation traffic islands and certain private gardens, much of today's popular gardening stems from Loudon's original philosophy, improved and interpreted by the great gardeners of the last 100 years.

In the modern age there was to be little more fancy landscaping on the lines of Brown and Repton. Much laying out and designing of small gardens was to be done and, more and more, the emphasis was on the beauty of the plants themselves. In the 1880s, the strong backlash against hard, formal planting was led by a gardener called William Robinson.

NO TO CARPET BEDDING

Born in Ireland in 1838, Robinson worked in a number of Irish gardens before crossing the sea in 1861 to take up work in Regents

Robinson's rose garden at Gravetye Manor. The planting is fairly relaxed by the standards of the early 20th century.

Robinson's specially converted Citroën. This enabled him to be driven to the less accessible parts of his Gravetye Estate.

WILLIAM ROBINSON

A Return to "Natural" Gardening

—1838—
Born in Ireland; later worked at various gardens, rising to the position of foreman

—1861—
Went to Regents Park, London

—1867—
Went to Paris as garden correspondent for The Times

—1868—
Visited the Alps

—1870—
Published Alpine Flowers for Gardens *and* The Wild Garden; *visited North America*

—1872—
The Garden *magazine launched*

—1879—
Gardening Illustrated *magazine launched*

—1883—
Gravetye Manor purchased. The English Flower Garden *published; further publications over next 40 years*

—1909—
Disabled by a bad fall

—1935—
Died

Park, London. By this time, the mania for carpet bedding was at its height in England. Encouraged by trend setters like Joseph Paxton, ostentation and artificiality ruled. Gardens were laid out in great wodges of lurid colours, punctuated by bushes clipped into peculiar shapes and surrounded by banks of depressing evergreens. Obelisks, urns and curiosities abounded. Lingering in the garden was not enjoyable. It hurt your eyes and raddled your senses.

Robinson was a lover of wild flowers and of trees. In his lifetime he was to plant hundreds of thousands of them.[15] He was also to set the trend towards naturalistic planting. He did not go all the way — indeed, by later standards, some of his planting was formalized — but he did begin the revolt against a form of gardening that was contrived and selfconscious.

His origins were humble[4]. He probably received little education but, by the time he moved to England, in his early twenties, he was an experienced foreman. At Regents Park he was put in charge of the herbaceous section, and was promoted rapidly. He began to collect wild flowers and, on country excursions, became familiar with the English cottages. He delighted in the jumble of plants in their gardens — herbs, fruit and flowers all apparently planted without any special design and yet all with specific uses. His observations inspired him to begin a career of garden writing.

He had provided *The Gardener's Chronicle* with several articles by 1867 when *The Times* sent him to Paris as a special correspondent. He wrote about French parks and gardens and later, after a tour of the Alps, published *Alpine Flowers for Gardens* (1870). More books followed quickly: *The Wild Garden* (1870), *Hardy Flowers* (1870) and *The Subtropical Garden* (1871).

Robinson's early work was not heavily critical of "formal" French parkmanship. However, as the years went by, his output became more abrasive until it developed into a crusade against what he called "straitlaced" and "mechanical", and in favour of "natural" style. He wrote:

> *I am a flower gardener, and not a mere spreader about of bad carpets done in reluctant flowers.*

In this respect Robinson and the Loudons had much in common. Loudon wrote copious notes about hedgerow flowers and cultivated florists' varieties in his garden, detesting what he called "tawdry" displays.

Robinson began several magazines. In 1872, after a trip to North America, he launched *The Garden*, which was financially disappointing but enabled him to further his crusade. *Gardening Illustrated* began in 1879 and was to run until 1956, when it merged with *Gardener's Chronicle*. Several other periodicals were produced during his life. In 1883 his most important work, *The English Flower Garden*, was published; in revised editions, this remained in print for about 80 years. It promoted "natural" gardening:

> *One aim of this book is to uproot the idea that a flower garden must always be of set pattern on one side of the house.*

By now he was becoming one of the most influential voices in British horticulture. With his ill disguised attacks on individuals and their gardens, he was making enemies too. Even dead champions of the age were not exempt. He called Paxton's Crystal Palace garden "the fruit of a poor ambition to outdo another ugly extravagance — Versailles".[4]

By 1883 he was rich enough to buy a country estate, Gravetye Manor, Sussex. Here at last, after so many years of working in other people's gardens, he was able to put into practice much of his gardening philosophy. At Gravetye he created his natural garden. He used herbaceous perennials such as *Aster novae angliae* (see page 66) not only in borders but naturalized in grass among shrubs. He is usually credited with being the first to plant bulbs in grass, but Loudon did this in his lawn in Bayswater, [13] and it is hard to believe that grass in earlier years had not been studded with at least bluebells and fritillaries, if nothing else. Robinson was a lover of small plants —

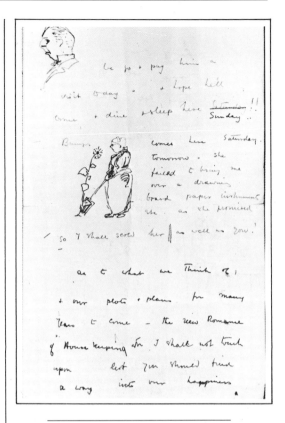

From a letter by Phipps, about 1906, a cartoon sketch of Gertrude Jekyll — nicknamed "Bumps" by Sir Edwin Lutyens.

Viola tricolor hybrids, walls planted with *Erinus* and yellow fumitory. In the fourth edition of *The Wild Garden* (1894) he describes a white *Clematis* growing up into a yew tree, a carpet of sweet cicely growing among shrubs, and roses growing into trees.

In 1909, at the age of 71, Robinson injured his back and was disabled. He continued to write and to travel about his estate in a specially converted vehicle.

Robinson's penchant for naturalism was also evident in Australia, championed by William Robert Guilfoyle, the man who created Melbourne's superb Botanic Gardens in their present form. Born in England, he migrated to Sydney with his family in 1853, cutting his teeth as a gardener in his father's Double Bay nursery. Guilfoyle's lifelong fascination with tropical plants was fired by a Pacific voyage aboard HMS *Challenger* as a naturalist in 1868 and by a subsequent spell developing a tropical garden in the Tweed River district of New South Wales, also growing tobacco and sugar cane.

In 1873 he succeeded the renowned explorer and plant hunter Ferdinand von Mueller as director of Melbourne's Botanic Gardens and embarked upon his life's work. The gardens had been laid out as a 2-hectare plot in 1846 and gradually enlarged by Mueller who sought to create a teaching garden, laying out plants in their "natural" botanic order.

Guilfoyle wrought radical changes. Inspired by such 18th-century masters of the "natural" style as Lancelot "Capability" Brown, he altered the entire landscape, uprooting and repositioning trees to open up broad vistas so that the gardens resembled the grounds of an English estate. Throughout the grounds clumps of flowering shrubs, rhododendrons, azaleas and camellias, added colour and broke up the landscape. It was a carefully contrived marriage of nature and artifice that

WILLIAM ROBERT GUILFOYLE
Australia's greatest Landscape Gardener

—1840—
Born December 8th at Chelsea, England

—1868—
Visited the Pacific as plant collector aboard HMS Challenger

—1869—
Moves to Tweed River, NSW, and establishes tropical garden

—1873—
Appointed director of Botanic Gardens Melbourne

—1874—
Published First Book of Australian Botany

—1880—
Published The ABC of Botany

—1890—
Visited England and Europe to inspect foreign gardens

—1909—
Retired as director of Botanic Gardens

—1911—
Published Australian Plants

—1912—
Died June 25

relished the unexpected, as Guilfoyle explained:

One of the greatest essentials in landscape gardening is the variety of foliage and disposal of trees. Nothing can excel the glimpses afforded by the openings between naturally formed clumps of trees and shrubs, whose height and contrast of foliage have been studied. At every step, the visitor finds some new view — something fresh, lively and striking, especially when tastefully arranged. Where long sombre rows of trees are planted, and a sameness of foliage exists, the very reverse is the case. Nature's most favourable aspects then seem sacrificed to art, and that art often produces but a chilling effect.

Such sentiments rejected the Victorian trend towards ornate formal layouts and vanquished the rather staid efforts of Guilfoyle's predecessor. By the time he retired in 1909, having twice toured the great gardens of Europe and Britain to seek inspiration and compare his achievements with those of other masters, Guilfoyle had won himself world acclaim by establishing Melbourne's Botanic Gardens as one of the world's great public parks.

"MISS BUMPS"

Robinson may have started the trend to naturalistic gardening but Gertrude Jekyll perfected the style. Robinson and Jekyll were

The gardens at Hestercombe, Somerset —
another product of the Jekyll-Lutyens
partnership.

friends for many years and worked together on
The Garden, which she edited for a short time
when he stood down. There is no doubt that
the two horticulturists influenced each other,
although it is not clear who had the greater
effect upon whom.

It is fashionable today to rank Jekyll as one
of the greatest figures in the history of horticulture. That she has had a profound influence on
modern gardening is indisputable. Her colour
schemes, her plant associations, her treatment
of wild gardens and her approach to garden
layout can be seen everywhere. Her long association with Sir Edwin Lutyens, the architect, is
hailed by many as a triumphant coming
together of ideas. Looking at it another way,
one could suggest that Jekyll managed some
pretty successful planting schemes in spite of
an excess of garden architecture. Without
doubt, her sense of artistry shone through her
plant groups regardless of whether they were
in a constructed garden or in a tract of unspoilt
woodland.

Her parents were wealthy and respected
but had no time for the strictures of the Victorian age. They allowed her to attend art school
(female students were rare), where she
learned to become a competent artist and
craftsman. She managed to get a painting into
the Royal Academy and, encouraged by a
good friendship with William Morris, began to
work on embroidery, woodcarving and even
silverwork.[16]

She travelled extensively, and assisted with
interiors for such places as Girton College and
the Duke of Westminster's Eaton Hall. Besides
Morris, her friends included Ruskin, Burne
Jones and Brabazon — who taught her some of
her colour sense. She was evidently a member
of the artistic set. She never married; and
because of her tubby stature was nicknamed
"Bumps" by Edwin Lutyens.

Poor eyesight was a serious weakness. She must have known that her eyes were deteriorating, because in 1891 she consulted a Dr Pagenstecher in Wiesbaden, who announced what must have sounded like a heavy penal sentence. She was told that, unless she stopped all close work — all embroidery and painting — her sight would fail. Although this did not mean financial ruin, it did prevent her from pursuing her career.

It was at this point in her life that she turned her attention to gardening. She began to write copiously — history fails to relate why it was safe for her to write but not to paint or embroider! — and to design planting schemes. By now her partnership with Lutyens was developing.

Jekyll's genius lay in her ability to place the right plants together. She was able to combine their different characteristics — not only their colours — to create an artistic whole, much as any artist makes use of the materials at his or her disposal. To do this successfully is more difficult than it sounds, and even in the best gardens there are near misses; elsewhere there are disasters. In her *Colour in the Flower Garden* (1908) she wrote:

> *Having got the plants, the great thing is to use them with careful selection and definite intention. Merely having them planted unassorted in garden spaces, is only like having a box of paints from the best colourman.*

GERTRUDE JEKYLL

Painter turned Gardener

—1843—
Born November 29th in London

—1848—
Moved to Bramley, Surrey

—1861—
Entered Kensington School of Art

—1866—
Had painting accepted for Summer Exhibition, Royal Academy of Arts

—1868—
Moved to Wargrave Hill, Berkshire

—1875—
Association with William Robinson began

—1876—
Father died. Moved to Munstead Heath

—1889—
Association with Sir Edwin Lutyens began

—1891—
Crisis with her eyesight

—1896—
New house at Munstead Wood begun

—1900—
Published Home and Garden, *to be followed by many more books over the years*

—1908—
Published Colour in the Flower Garden

—1932—
Died (December 8th)

In her own garden at Munstead Wood in Surrey she was careful to retain as much woodland as possible, thinning trees here and there until groups and walks were left. She planted the shaded areas with woodland plants — hellebores, primroses, anemones and bulbs. Her 'Munstead Bunch' primroses (a range of polyanthuses from white to deep gold) were developed, not by a technical plant-breeding programme, but simply by collecting and sowing seed from the best plants.

THE LUTYENS / JEKYLL PARTNERSHIP

The value of her association with Lutyens is difficult to assess. In gardening there are two extremes of opinion. On the one side, the plantsman argues that a garden's most important function is to serve as a repository of plants. Like butterflies in a cabinet, the effect is more pleasing if they are arranged in some sort of order, but artefacts and edifices are acceptable only if they serve to accommodate the plants. The other extreme is to suggest that a garden is an extension of the house and, as such, is an integral part of the architecture. Plants, where they are used, must not interfere with the architect's line.

Jekyll's approach was based firmly upon a knowledge and understanding of each plant's individuality. She was a highly observant plantswoman, despite her visual handicap, and she based her planting on purely natural principles. Lutyens was designing buildings for an empire. His boulevards in New Delhi are a manifestation of the arrogance of that era. Many of his "landscape" designs are equally selfconscious. For example, at Marsh Court, Hampshire, he made a sunken garden with hundreds of steps, a score or so of small, raised terraced beds, yards of balustrade and a rectangular pond. Nobody, not even Jekyll, would be able to soften this rigid layout with naturalistic planting. And yet the restriction of planting area seems, strangely, to work. There are many good examples of gardens which, although they are not carried to Lutyens' extremes, rely on rigid formal layout within which planting is based upon Jekyll lines. (Sissinghurst Castle in Kent, discussed below, is probably the finest example.) The Jekyll-Lutyens partnership continued for many years, during which more than 100 gardens were planned.

Photography became one of Jekyll's hobbies, and this must have provided some small compensation for her being unable to paint. She certainly took some good pictures, developing and processing the plates herself.[16] Her books continued to appear, and she wrote for various periodicals. All her gardening advice was based on her own practical experience. She was quite used to hard physical work and, although there was no shortage of skilled labour at Munstead Wood, she did a great deal of the gardening herself. Her love of flowers was all-embracing. She had as much affection for the humblest as

VITA SACKVILLE-WEST

A Turbulent Life: a Tranquil Garden

—1892—
Born at Knole, Kent

—1913—
Married Harold Nicolson. Restored garden at Cospoli, Turkey

—1914—
First son born

—from 1915—
Developed garden at Long Barn, Kent

—1917—
Nigel Nicolson born

—1926—
Published The Land

—1929—
Nicolson left diplomatic service

—1930—
Bought Sissinghurst Castle

—1933—
Gave her first garden talk on radio

—1946—
Began regular garden column in The Observer *(ran until 1961)*

—1949—
Elected to National Trust Garden Committee

—1962—
Died

for the grandest. See what she says of London pride:

> *When its pink cloud of bloom is at its best, I always think it the prettiest thing in the garden.*[17]

Of *Gypsophila*:

> *Its delicate masses of bloom are like clouds of flowery mist settled down upon the flower borders.*

And even of Elder:

> *I am very fond of the elder-tree. It is a sociable sort of thing.*

SELF-TAUGHT EXPERTS

Gertrude Jekyll lived to be almost 90. She was still writing a few weeks before she died. To this day, her influence is universal. We are all, to some extent, ruled by her colour schemes, her plant associations, her passion for simple flowers and her dislike of "overdoing" things. Examples of Jekyll-inspired gardens abound everywhere. Vita Sackville-West, although she met Jekyll only once, was probably deeply influenced by her. Her garden at Sissinghurst certainly bears all the Jekyll trademarks, even though the two women were not in direct communication. As Robinson and Jekyll are among the most prominent horticulturists of the day, it would have been unlikely for any gardener in the early part of the 20th century not to have been influenced by them.

Victoria (Vita) Sackville-West

led such a strange life that it is easy to become fascinated with her biography and forget about her plants. She was decidedly upper-crust — her father was Lord Sackville. She was born at Knole, which is a 400 hectares estate on the edge of Sevenoaks, Kent. Her parents were cousins, each of whom had affairs, and they separated. Her mother became mentally ill towards the end of her life.

The house at Knole is enormous, with the parkland running up to lawns and then the lawns running up to the house. Vita's only gardening in her childhood and youth consisted of sowing cress on a wet flannel and growing a few childish vegetables.[18] She married Harold Nicolson, son of Lord Carnock and nephew of the Viceroy of India (Lord Dufferin), at Knole in October 1913. Nicolson was a diplomat, and they moved straight to Turkey where, at Cospoli, they began to develop their first garden. They had very little time there, however, for Nicolson was recalled in 1914.

In 1915 they bought Long Barn, a cottage quite close to Knole. It was a mess. The house was in poor condition and the land was piled with rubble and weeds. They set to work, repairing the house and creating a garden from the chaos outside. At this stage, Sackville-West knew nothing at all about gardening or plants. She wrote in her notebook: "When and how to plant lilac? When wild thyme? Wild sedums? ... What other good rock things, bushy? Good climbing roses?"[18] However, within a few years she had served an energetic apprenticeship and had absorbed enough knowledge to be able to grow most things successfully. She was especially fond of wild flowers and planned, at Long Barn, wild rose and honeysuckle in the hedges and wild cherry in the copse.

At the end of World War I, their private lives were in disarray. Harold had become infected from a homosexual adventure and Vita had an affair with Violet Keppel, daughter of one of Edward VII's mistresses. The two women took

The Nicolsons created the gardens at Sissinghurst from a ruin. This is the so-called cottage garden in the grounds.

a number of holidays together over a three-year period. In the meantime, Violet Keppel married Denys Trefusis but resumed her relationship with Sackville-West. Eventually, the affair fizzled out, but there were other affairs with other women — including Virginia Woolf. Nicolson and Sackville-West patched things up and their marriage, such as it was, continued.

In 1926 Sackville-West published a long poem, *The Land*, which was critically acclaimed and won her the Hawthornden Prize for Literature. She wrote a number of other works of both poetry and prose.

DERELICTION TO DELECTATION

In 1929, when development was threatened near Long Barn, the Nicolsons went house-hunting. Near Sissinghurst, Kent, they looked

Roundel hedges, seen from the tower at
Sissinghurst Castle.

at a wrecked Elizabethan building, a huddle of
broken-down farm buildings and an odd-
looking tower. For this assortment, plus 200
hectares of land they paid £12,000. By today's
standards this may sound cheap, but it was not.

The property needed £15,000 spending on
it, and even then accommodation was likely to
be inconvenient. However, the place had distant family connections and, as Nicolson wrote
to Vita, in part:

> *c) It is in Kent. It is a part of Kent we
> like. It is self contained, I could make a
> lake. The boys could ride.*
> *d) We like it.*

From then onwards, the Nicolsons spent
much of their time and energy creating, out of
this delapidated site, one of the finest gardens
in the country. Nicolson was the designer. His

ideas of line and contour were impeccable. His
was the rounded hedge, his the pleached lime
walk where the spring garden was to be. He
had a lot going for him. Sissinghurst Castle was
full of old, mellow brick walls and courtyards, a
dry moat and lots of different levels. By laying
out a crafty network of hedges he was able to
divide the area into different zones, each inde-
pendent, but each clearly leading to the next.

Vita Sackville-West, with ten years' experience at Long Barn behind her, became the
plantswoman. There is a great deal of Jekyll in
her planting, particularly in her use of colour.
Her triumph is the rose garden, where she fos-
tered many varieties of old rose that had gone
so far out of fashion they were in danger of
extinction. She and Nicolson rescued one
unfamiliar rose which was growing in the rub-
bish when they moved in; it was thought by
some to be 'Rose de Maures', previously considered extinct, and was reintroduced as 'Sissinghurst Castle'.

She used a variety of plants in association
with the roses: irises, dittany and *Alchemilla*.
She planted *Allium albopilosum*, whose lav-
ender-mauve flowers go so well with the blush
shades of the old roses, and whose bold,
globe-shaped seed-heads keep the interest
going after the roses have finished.

She laid out a white garden — very Jekyll! —
with brick paths and centred by a huge
umbrella of *Rosa longicuspis* which is dazzling
in June. To heighten the whiteness she planted
silver-foliaged subjects and covered every inch
of soil with ground-cover — white comfrey and
white *Pulmonaria*.

From 1946 onwards, Sackville-West wrote a
regular column for *The Observer*. By now she
was recognized as a leading figure in horticultural circles. Her readers, although they may
not have aspired to making their own Sissing-
hursts, were able to identify with her. For
example, on the universal problem of sparrows
attacking primrose flowers, she wrote:

Has any reader of these articles a sovereign remedy against this naughty, wanton, wild destruction? ... This is a real S.O.S. I have quite a collection of uncommon primroses, Jack in the Green, Madame Pompadour, Cloth of Gold, and so on but what is the good of that if the sparrows take them all?

Nobody provided an efficacious cure. Someone even suggested Christian Science.[15]

By 1961 Sissinghurst was open to the public regularly, and was a delight to stroll through at any time of the year. Vita Sackville-West, now nearly 70, was forced to give up her writing because of illness. She died of cancer in 1962. The garden belongs to the National Trust, who maintain it, as faithfully as possible

Modern gardening along naturalistic lines is successful only when a rich variety of interesting plants is grown. The Nicolsons and Gertrude Jekyll enjoyed plenty of choice but, since their passing, we have benefited from an almost endless supply of new hybrids and new introductions of wild plants from all over the world. Throughout gardening history, keen collectors have always played an all-important role. Their work is all the more useful when based on practical trials in their own gardens.

CROCUSES, SNOWDROPS AND TULIP TEAS

There were many important collectors at the beginning of the 20th

E.A. BOWLES

The Last Great Plantsman

—1865—
Born May 14th, Myddelton House, London

—1889—
Visited Italy and collected first plants

—1900—
Elected to Scientific Committee, Royal Horticultural Society (Crocus *specialist*)

—1908—
Elected to Council of Royal Horticultural Society

—1910—
Discovered Primula bowlesii*; made frequent alpine trips over the years*

—1914—
Published My Garden in Spring *and* My Garden in Summer

—1915—
Published My Garden in Autumn and Winter

—1923—
Published A Handbook of Crocus and Colchicum for Gardeners

—1934—
Published A Handbook of Narcissus*; technical collaboration with Stearn on anemones and Stern on snowdrops*

—1954—
Died (May 7th)

One of Bowles' illustrations, painted in 1917, of a hybrid of *Galanthus plicatus* and *G. elwesii.*

century — men like E.H. Wilson, Reginald Farrer, William Purdom and Frank Kingdon-Ward — but one who was not only a collector but a fine gardener as well was E.A. Bowles. Whenever anyone begins to develop a burning interest in garden plants — something which can happen at almost any age — it is not long before the name "Bowles" crops up. Take any nursery catalogue, visit any public garden or leaf through any book about gardening and, sooner or later, you will find at least one plant named after him. Think of *Viola* 'Bowles Black', *Crocus chrysanthus* 'E.A Bowles', *Cheiranthus* 'Bowles Mauve' or *Cyclamen hederifolium* 'Bowles Apollo'.

Edward Augustus Bowles was born, lived and died in the same house. He was never short of money and never had to earn a living. Many in his position would have contributed little to society but, not counting his extensive work for charity, Bowles provided horticulture with a superb legacy of plants. His garden writing is steeped with expertise but at the same time entertains. His rugged support of the Royal Horticultural Society over half a century has been too valuable to calculate.

In the early 18th century Sir Hugh Myddelton constructed a "New River" to carry sweet water to the mushrooming population of London. Bowles' father was the last governor of the New River Company, and lived in the handsome and roomy Myddelton House on the riverbank. The company held its board meetings at the house, and young Bowles was befriended by one of the board members, Canon Henry Ellacombe, who was a knowledgeable plantsman and garden writer. Bowles, having decided to take Holy Orders, had read theology at Cambridge and was embarking on a course at theological college when his elder brother died of tuberculosis; his younger sister also caught the disease, and died soon afterwards. Bowles abandoned his training and returned to look after his bereaved parents.[15] Although he never became a priest, he was thereafter to work industriously at many pastoral duties. He ran a night school for boys as well as a Sunday school, and he took on far more than his fair share of parish duties.

He began plant-hunting abroad in his early twenties, becoming especially interested in the genus *Crocus*. By 1901 he was growing 135 species and varieties of crocus in open frames.[15] He became a close friend of Reginald Farrer (practically the father of modern rock gardening) and shared his enthusiasm for alpines. Bowles' rock garden at Myddelton House had to be big enough to house a wide and growing collection of alpine shrubs such as *Daphne col-*

lina as well as tiny plants and bulbs of all sizes from snowdrops to the tall and graceful *Dierama pulcherrimum* (see page 90). As an asthmatic and hay-fever sufferer, Bowles was in the habit of taking off for the mountains at the time of year when pollen counts in London reach their peak.

In 1900, because of his work with crocuses, he was invited to join the Royal Horticultural Society Scientific Committee — quite an honour for someone in his early thirties with no scientific qualifications! He served the society diligently and in 1908 was elected to its Council. He attended meetings for 45 more years. In 1917 the society awarded him the Victoria Medal of Honour.

Bowles' strength was in his ability to identify a plant quickly and accurately. Although, like Gertrude Jekyll, his eyesight was by no means perfect, he had acute powers of observation. As a talented artist he was able to illustrate his own books on crocuses, *Colchicum* and daffodils. His drawings are not only botanically accurate, they are a delight to look at. He was an amateur, untrained botanist, but this was no disadvantage. Indeed, the cold science of botany was a little hard for him to take at times. When working with Sir Frederick Stern on a book about the genus *Galanthus* (snowdrops), he found the technical approach so irksome that his contribution was restricted to a chapter on how to grow them in gardens.

His main contribution to garden literature was the trilogy *My Garden in Spring* (1914), *My Garden in Summer* (1914) and *My Garden in Autumn and Winter* (1915). The works are packed with useful information, but they are also humorous and entertaining. As a reader you are conducted round the garden with Bowles' gentle commentary flowing as you go. His powers of observation show you things you would never have noticed. Take his description of the scent of *Cytisus battandieri*:

Sometimes it reminds me of strawberries, and at others of grapefruit and lemons, or of a fruit salad with a dash of maraschino or kirsch. You can get all these scents from the same bunch of blooms at different times of the day.[15]

The sunken garden at Hampton Court beautifully maintained today, showing modern tulips used as carpet bedding.

Bowles was one of the few men to see the funny side of some plants. He even had what he called a "lunatic asylum", for plants that had gone off their rockers: black pansies, oak-leaved laburnum, evergreen elder and twisted hazel. His garden may not have exhibited the finest landscaping, but it certainly held one of the most exciting collections of plants this century has seen in private hands.

Living on, gardening to a ripe old age, Bowles was popular and respected. The church fêtes at Myddelton must have provided a wonderful excuse for budding plantsmen to browse in this little paradise. Every year on his birthday a "Tulip Tea" was given. The tulips were grown in a series of raised beds along the New River, each bed underplanted with massed forget-me-nots. In his late eighties, although still active, he began to have heart trouble. The frail old gentleman managed to sit on a Royal Horticultural Society Floral Committee meeting for the last time in April 1954. He died the following month, a few days before his 89th birthday.

A-Z
DIRECTORY OF PLANTS

*I*N the first section of this book, devoted to the great horticulturists and botanists, we have seen evidence of a developing awareness of the central importance of plants to Man's physical and emotional well-being (as balm both for the sick body and the restless soul), and that this awareness prompted a strong urge for enlightenment. In different centuries the desire for knowledge has taken various forms: in the early days it was the medicinal properties of plants which absorbed the energies of educated minds whereas, by the late 18th century, aesthetic considerations coupled with the search for successful cultivation techniques, rose in the scale of priorities. This last is demonstrated by the single-minded pursuit of excellence in a narrow field as characterized by the growers of "florist's flowers", such as the auricula and the pansy. By the 1870s, the emphasis had shifted towards finding good garden-worthy plants in preference to those which were medicinally important or interesting only to the "florist". Plant hunters went out from Europe to search all over the world for plants to adorn gardens and glasshouses. Plant-collecting reached its peak in the early years of the 20th century. The wealth of plant material available today is, in part, a tribute to the determination and courage of plant collectors over the last 150 years, and the immense lengths to which rational people will go to in pursuit of a praiseworthy goal.

Many of the species described in the A-Z Direc-tory, such as the pomegranate and the Madonna Lily, have been cultivated for thousands of years. For those who believe that the enjoyment of gardening lies not solely (or even principally) in the practical cultivation of plants, but also in the aggregation of information which concerns them, the origins and history of these plants is undoubtedly fascinating. Any stroll around the garden, especially if shared with friends, becomes all the more precious and rewarding.

The fifty plants in the A-Z Directory all have some connection with the horticulturists, plant collectors and botanists featured in the first section of the book: they have either been discovered by, written about, or grown by these enlightened men and women. Each entry contains information about how the plant reached us (where applicable), whom we can thank for it, its culinary or medicinal uses, and any stories or legends which are connected with it. A short description of the plant is given, and is written with the general-interest reader as well as the gardener or botanist in mind. Interesting hybrids or forms grown in gardens today are also mentioned here. Practical advice for the gardener is given in the form of a short account of the best means of cultivating the plant, its preferences in the way of soil and aspect, as well as the best means of propagating it. Lastly, there is a quick reference section on the main features of the plant: its size, flowering time, flower colour and scent.

ACACIA BAILEYANA

Cootamundra Wattle

AUSTRALIA'S national flower is well represented by some 600 species, ranging from large trees to small shrubs. All are evergreen, and many feature briliant yellow or gold blossoms in late spring and summer. The first acacias to reach Europe from Australia were collected by the Kew plant hunter David Nelson, who is honoured by *Acacia verticillata,* Nelson's Mimosa. Other species were dispatched by another Kew man and Joseph Banks' protege, George Caley, who arrived in New South Wales in 1797 and spend 10 years exploring the hinterland and collecting plant species, including *A. podalyriifolia,* originally known as *A. caleyi.* Today the most popular and widely grown garden species is probably *A. baileyana.* Originally found around the Cootamundra district of southern New South Wales, the Cootamundra Wattle commemorates Frederick Manson Bailey, an English botanist who migrated to South Australia and, after a sojourn as an orchardist in New Zealand, eventually settled in Queensland where he was appointed Colonial Botanist in 1881, writing numerous botanical papers and books, including the six-volume magus opus *The Queensland Flora* (1889-1906).

A. *baileyana* is characterized by a spectacular show of fluffy ball-shaped golden blossoms that appear in winter and spring. This species has a thick canopy of feathery silver-grey leaves and is sometimes confused with *A. dealbata,* commonly known as the Silver Wattle. Young specimens of *A. baileyana* are identifiable by their pyramid shape, with branches trailing the ground, while mature trees feature a dense crown of leaves topping a short trunk.

CULTIVATION

Although, like many Australian natives, *A. baileyana* is capable of surviving very dry conditions it grows best when treated to generous and regular watering. It can be grown in a container from seed and transplanted to a well-drained location in fertile, slightly acid soil at any time of the year. This species is especially suited to mass plantings. *A. baileyana* should be protected from the wind and enjoys full sun, although it can tolerate partial shade. Like other acacias it is a fast-growing species and has a rather short life-span, usually stretching from 10 to 15 years, although this can sometimes be enhanced by judicious pruning after flowering. The previous season's growth should be cut back to two or three buds or shoots. It is particularly important to avoid cutting the older mature wood, unless it is decided to remove a branch altogether, so as not to discourage the development of new shoots. The plant should be mulched with garden compost or animal manure after pruning, and a complete fertilizer is best applied at the same time. Like all wattles *A. baileyana* is susceptible to borers.

FEATURES

Height: 6m after 10 years; 10m at maturity

Flowering period: Winter—summer

Colour: Golden-yellow

1 Stamens
2 Corolla
3 Pistil
4 Calyx

ACANTHUS MOLLIS

Bear's breeches; Oyster Plant

*T*HIS plant, which is a native of Italy and southern Europe, was known in Britain long before its introduction there in 1548. It soon became popular because of its supposed efficacy as a soother of burns, gout and stomach upsets. John Evelyn wrote that it was a "mollifying herbe" for "members out of yointe".

This is the plant whose leaves are depicted, in a stylized way, at the top of Corinthian columns. The story goes that the architect Callimachus (late 5th century BC), who was at the time building a a temple in Corinth, saw a plant of it growing under a basket on which had been placed a tile. Apparently the leaves had grown through the basket and been turned back by the tile. A picturesque story, but little credence need be given to it.

In 1551, William Turner noted in his *New Herbal* that

> *this herbe groweth plentifully in my Lordes [Somerset] garden at Sion [Syon Park]. I never saw it grow wilde as yet [It was not found wild in England until 1820] . . . They that will have anye more of the description of Branke Ursine [bear's claw] let them rede the description of Dioscorides . . . which I do nowe pass over because I know that the herbe is so perfitelye knowen in all countries.*

It may not be "so perfitelye knowen" to all as, until recently, it was not widely grown. The fashion for planting striking "architectural" plants however, has brought it once more to public notice and acclaim. William Robinson, for example, called it "long neglected" in his *The English Flower Garden* of 1883. An herbaceous perennial, *A. mollis* has large, mid-green, shiny, pendulous, deeply indented leaves between 45cm and 1m long. The flowers, on long, upright spikes, are white with purple hoods (bracts). It is a most stately and imposing plant.

CULTIVATION

This plant is not difficult to grow, provided that one leaves it to its own devices and resists all temptation to move it around. It is happiest left in peace in either a sunny or a partially shaded place in a deep, well drained soil. It benefits from ample and regular watering in summer. The soil need not be rich, but it should be deep because the roots will venture down a long way. *A. mollis* can be propagated quite easily by division in late autumn or by taking root cuttings in winter. A liquid fertilizer should be applied twice each year.

FEATURES

Height: 2m
Flowering period: Summer
Colour: White and purple flowers; glossy green leaves.

1 Petal
2 Style
3 Stamen
4 Sepal

AGAPANTHUS AFRICANUS (A. UMBELLATUS)

African Lily

*T*HIS was introduced to Britain from the Cape Province of South Africa as early as 1629. The first illustration of it, dated 1692, is by Plunkenet; the model for his illustration was flowering at Hampton Court, and so may well have been imported by the nursery firm of London and Wise. The nomenclature is a little uncertain, having changed from *A. africanus* to *A. umbellatus* and back again. The species has long been a favourite of Australian gardeners, partly because it is easy to grow.

The African Lily is a hardy perennial with fleshy roots, and flowers (up to 30 in an umbel) which are borne on the end of long succulent stems above a clump of strap-shaped evergreen leaves. The flowers are deep violet-blue and like an open bell in shape. Each plant bears scores of flower stems. *A. orientalis,* commonly known as the Lily of the Nile, is similar in appearance except that the umbel contains between 100 and 200 white or sky-blue flowers throughout summer.

CULTIVATION

Agapanthus does best in full sun and are often grown as borders, ground-cover and clumps in shrubbery. They are also suitable for growing in pots or tubs in the garden. They like a fertile, deep, but well-drained soil, and their crowns should be planted just below ground level in spring. Regular feeding with a liquid fertilizer in the growing season will encourage them to flower well. Frequent and thorough watering throughout the growing season is also important.

They are best and most easily propagated by division in winter as they readily make offsets, which can be detached. Old flowers and leaves should be removed in autumn.

FEATURES

Height: 60cm
Flowering period: Summer
Colour: Deep blue-violet

1 Petal
2 Stamen
3 Style
4 Ovary

ANEMONE ROBINSONIANA

Robinson's Windflower

ACCORDING to William Robinson (never a man to hide his light under a bushel) in *The Wild Garden* (1870):

> *The most beautiful form of our wood Anemone* [Anemone nemerosa] *which has come into the garden in our day is the large sky-blue form. I first saw it as a small tuft at Oxford* [Oxford Botanic Garden] *and grew it in London where it was often seen with me in bloom by Mr. Boswell Syme, author of the Third Edition of Sowerby* [James Sowerby's English Botany, *first published in 36 volumes, from 1790 to 1814*]. . . *and we were often struck with its singular charm about noon on bright days. There is reason to believe that there is both in England and Ireland a large and handsome form of the wood Anemone — distinct from the common white of our woods and shaws* [small woods] *in spring, and that my blue Anemone is a variety of this. It is not the same as the blue form wild in parts of North Wales and elsewhere in Britain, this being more fragile looking and not so light a blue.*

He thought it useful for the rock-garden, for the edges of borders, for the wild garden beneath shrubs and for naturalizing in grass.

E.A. Bowles believed that *A. robinsoniania* arose not from Ireland but from Norway, via ireland. Being something of a botanical sleuth he was probably right.

A. robinsoniana has flowers which are more than 2.5cm across and lavender-blue; the petals have edges which are slightly undulated. It has leaves which are cut into three segments and very deeply toothed. This species may be difficult to find in Australia and New Zealand. *A. japonica,* which grows to 1.5m and has white flowers, and *A. blanda,* which usually has white flowers with black centres, are more common species.

CULTIVATION

Closely connected as it is to *A. nemerosa, A. robinsoniana* revels in moist conditions in rich soil and needs to be well watered in dry periods. It is best grown in part shade, preferably under trees. A complete fertilizer should be applied in winter. Propagation is by seeds sown in late summer or, more commonly, from bulbs planted in autumn. Anemones can fall prey to snails and hematodes.

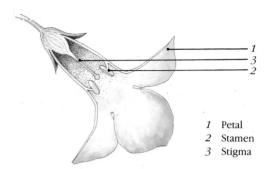

FEATURES

Height: 15-20cm
Flowering period: Summer
Colour: Lavender blue

1 Petal
2 Stamen
3 Stigma

AQUILEGIA CANADENSIS

Columbine; Granny's Bonnet

AQUILEGIA CANADENSIS was the first aquilegia to be introduced to Britain. It comes from northern North America, and its introduction is one of the results of the fruitful plant-hunting trip which John Tradescant the younger made to Virginia in 1637. It differs from *A. vulgaris* (described below) in having yellow flowers with red spurs to the petals. Linnaeus was the first person to discover that these spurs contained the plant's nectaries. The flowers are up to 4cm across and 1cm long, with longer spurs, and come out in spring. The leaves are in three parts and dark green. Like all other columbines, *A. canadensis* hybridizes promiscuously with others in the garden. There is a dwarf form, *A.c.* var. *nana,* as well as a paler yellow version called *flavescens. A vulgaris,* which has fern-like leaves and purple, pink, white, lavender, cream or yellow flowers depending on type, is the most commonly grown Columbine in Australia and New Zealand.

CULTIVATION

A. canadensis enjoys a moist, but not waterlogged, soil in sun or a little shade. A complete fertilizer should be applied shortly after planting. Like all columbines, it will hybridize with others easily, so the stems need to be cut down after flowering to prevent that. It is best propagated by sowing the seed autumn or spring in seed trays, which can be put in a cold frame; the seedlings can then be pricked out when large enough to handle. Division is possible in the dormant season if you wish to avoid any hybridization. Aquilegias are occasionally bothered by aphids but are otherwise reasonably trouble-free.

FEATURES

Height: 30-60cm
Flowering period: Spring
Colour: Yellow with red spurs

1 Sepal
2 Ovary
3 Petal
4 Stigma
5 Stamen

ARBUTUS UNEDO

Irish Strawberry Tree

*A*RBUTUS UNEDO has a most interesting history. It is a native of the Mediterranean region and Asia Minor (where its berries are used to make preserves and alcoholic drinks, and the bark, leaves and fruit are used for tanning) as well as of the southwest of Ireland, around the Lakes of Killarney. There is a story to explain why this has come about: the tree appeared in Ireland as a miracle to remind the monk Bresal of the time he had spent in Spain teaching the Spanish monks Irish choral music. Appealing as this explanation is, it is more likely that the arbutus grew all over Europe just after the last retreat of the glaciers (about 10,000 years ago), when the climate was warmer than it is now, but that, as temperatures cooled in northern Europe, it survived in only a few places.

This arbutus was described by William Turner in 1548, and by 1759 Philip Miller was listing not only a red-flowered kind but also double-flowered varieties. Parkinson remarked that the colour of the fruits was like a "pallide clarret wine".

The plant's species name, *unedo*, means "one I eat"; this refers to the fruits of the plant. Although these are edible, they are not sufficiently nice to tempt anyone to eat more than one. Other varieties include *A. menziesii*, the Madrona of California, which has smooth cinnamon-coloured bark that peels off in large flakes, and *A. andrachne*, the Grecian Strawberry Tree.

A. unedo fruits at the same time as it flowers, which makes it a most valuable ornamental shrub or small tree. The flowers are white and hang in short pendant panicles. The small round fruits are initially green, then yellow and finally bright orange-red hence *A. unedo's* common name, the Strawberry Tree. This tree, has torn deep red-brown bark and elliptical or oval leaves up to 10cm in length, which taper at both ends. The leaves are smooth and dark green.

CULTIVATION

In general terms *Arbutus* are not happy on alkaline soils, but *A. unedo,* which is found wild on limy soil in Yugoslavia, is an exception. All *Arbutus* species require a sunny position in a deep well-drained soil. Regular and thorough watering is necessary, and poor soil should be improved with leafmould, peat moss or sand. The plant is wind-resistant, but salt carried by sea breezes can burn the flowers and leaves. *A. unedo* can be planted from a container at any time of the year and is usually propagated by seed in spring. If a fertilizer is used a balanced solution should be applied in spring and summer. It may be necessary to spray for aphids. *A. unedo* does not generally need pruning.

FEATURES

Height: Up to 6m
Flowering period: Autumn and winter
Colour: White; fruits orange-red.

1   Stigma
2   Sepal
3   Petal

ASTER NOVAE-ANGLIAE

New England Aster; Easter Daisy

*M*ORE than 500 species exist in this massive genus, which is native to all continents except Australia, where the plants are popular as herbaceous perennials. Although there are numerous individual names the genus is commonly referred to as either the Michaelmas Daisy, in the northern hemisphere, or the Easter Daisy, in the southern hemisphere. This popular name owes its origin to the introduction of the Gregorian calendar into Britain in 1752. The new calendar meant that Michaelmas (September 29th) now fell 11 days earlier and began to coincide with the time that the aster was flowering. Of course, south of the equator they bloom around Easter.

As its name suggests, *A. novae-angliae* comes from New England. It has drab green lanceolate leaves growing thickly along the stems and features clusters of pink or violet-purple daisy-like blooms throughout summer. The flowers range from 2.5cm to 5cm in diameter. *A. novi-belgii,* a favourite species in Australia, is the parent of most of the commonly grown hybrids, and its multi-petalled blooms vary in colour from purple and crimson, through pink, mauve, blue and white. *A. dumosus,* the Dwarf Michaelmas Daisy, grows up to 20cm in height and has pale mauve flowers.

CULTIVATION

Asters like a well-drained but not droughty soil which is well dug with organic material such as leaf mould or peat. They prefer sun, although they will stand a little shade in very hot areas. They usually need staking, as well as mulching in spring to prevent the soil drying out. A liquid fertilizer should be applied annually. *A. novae-angliae* has not the need for annual division which makes *A. novi-belgii* rather a nuisance to grow, but it should be divided every three years in the dormant season. When the plant is being divided, the middle piece should be thrown away and only the younger outside buds replanted. Asters can be grown from seeds planted in seed boxes throughout spring and early summer. When transplanted they should be bedded 20 to 30cm apart. A mulch of lawn clippings is best spread over the seedlings in hot weather to preserve moisture and keep the roots cool. Plants flower four to five months after sowing. Slugs like them, as do aphids. The plant should be cut back to ground level soon after flowering.

FEATURES

Height: 1.5m
Flowering period: Late summer
Colour: Pink or violet-purple.

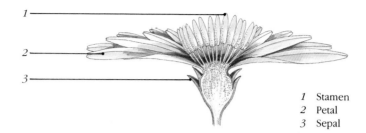

1 Stamen
2 Petal
3 Sepal

BANKSIA SERRATA

Red Honeysuckle; Saw Banksia

WHEN James Cook made his first landfall on the east coast of Australia in 1770 the *Endeavour's* botanists, Joseph Banks and Daniel Solander, were so overwhelmed by the variety of new species that they encountered while foraging amongst the coastal sandhills and scrub that they named the place Botany Bay. Among the species they catalogued was an entirely new genus, Banks' namesake, the *Banksia,* which contains some 50 species of evergreen shrub or small tree native to Australia. Members of this genus are characterized by gnarled trunks and rough bark, thick, mostly narrow leaves, and slender flowers grouped cylindrically on long brush-like cones. The flowers range in colour through red, orange, yellow and greenish white and are often used in dried flower arrangements. The first banksias to reach the outside world were *Banksia integrifolia* and *B. ericifolia,* dispatched to Kew in 1788 by the first governor of the infant colony of New South Wales, Arthur Phillip.

One of the most popular garden species is *B. serrata,* an especially gnarled plant with red flower spikes which turn into woody cones as the seeds set. The cones were the inspiration for May Gibbs' banksia men, the villains of her enduring children's tale *The Adventures of Snugglepot and Cuddlepie* (1918). The flower spikes contain large amounts of nectar which produces dark and strongly flavoured honey, giving the species one of its common names, while the long, toothed leaves prompted the other.

CULTIVATION

The Red Honeysuckle thrives in poor well-drained sandy or light loamy soils and, although tolerant of dry spells, needs regular watering until established. It has a shallow, non-spreading root system and is ideally suited to containers. Alternatively it can be planted as a hedge or windbreak. It likes full or partial sun and should be fed with a slow-release fertilizer suited for native plants in spring. Propagation is by seed in autumn. In its natural state *B. serrata* and other members of this genus reproduce after bushfires, which split the seed pods. Like other natives it is susceptible to borers.

FEATURES

Height: 8m
Flowering period: Summer
Colour: Red

1 Stigma
2 Stamens
3 Corolla
4 Ovary
5 Style

BOUGAINVILLEA GLABRA

*N*AMED in honour of the French navigator Louis Antoine de Bougainville, who circumnavigated the world between 1766–1769, this magnificent evergreen climber, covered with brilliant imperial purple flower bracts in spring and summer, is a native of Brazil. The genus, which contains some dozen species, was introduced to Europe, where it was cultivated in greenhouses and conservatories, by Bougainville's naturalist Philibert de Commerson, who discovered it while foraging around Rio de Janeiro in 1768. Of the original species only two have become popular with gardeners, *Bougainvillia glabra* (also known as *B. magnifica traillii*) and *B. spectabilis,* although some two centuries of hybridization have produced several varieties that equal or surpass the parent stock. Colours vary from crimson and magenta purple through pink to bronze, cream, white and yellow. Bougainvillea does best in warm temperate or tropical conditions, although the species *B. glabra* is able to withstand cold conditions better than many varieties. However, in colder areas all bougainvillias should be protected from frost and grown in warm sunny locations. The plants have long hooked canes that can be trained to grow on almost any support, although they need assistance as they are not self-clinging. *B. glabra* has pointed green leaves, and the purple bracts enclose small creamy flowers. *B. spectabilis,* commonly known as 'Mrs Butt' and discovered in Columbia in the early 20th century, reaching Kew via Trinidad, has bracts that vary in colour from red through pink, white, cream and yellow.

CULTIVATION

B. glabra prefers sandy, well-drained soils that have been prepared with manure or compost and is best planted in warm weather. It should be kept dry in winter and although able to tolerate dry conditions growth is enhanced by regular watering in spring and summer. It enjoys full sun and needs protection from wind and frost in colder areas. A complete fertilizer should be applied in late spring and again during summer. Pruning of old growth is carried out during spring while propagation is from hardwood cuttings taken in spring or early summer.

FEATURES

Height: 6m
Flowering period: Spring and summer
Colour: Purple bracts surrounding cream flowers. Varieties and hybrids in many colours

1 Perianth
2 Stamens
3 Calyx
4 Ovary
5 Style

BUDDLEIA DAVIDII

Butterfly Bush; Summer Lilac

A native of China, *B. davidii* features long tube-like flowers in panicles and is much loved by butterflies and planted widely for that reason alone. But it is also a very handsome and hardy deciduous shrub.

It was first introduced to the West by Dr Augustine Henry, an Irish doctor who joined the Imperial Customs Service in China and lived for several years at Ichang. He named it after the French missionary Père David, who had firs found it there some years before. However, a better form was raised, by the French nursery, Vilmorin, from seed sent in 1893 by another missionary, Père Soulié. Père Soulié's fate is an instructive example of how dangerous plant-hunting can be: he was killed by bandits in 1905.

B. davidii makes a strong-growing bush, with grey-green lanceolate leaves and slightly arching panicles of scented lilac flowers, orange at the mouth, which come out in summer and autumn. These panicles can be as long as 20cm on vigorous plants. Numerous good forms have been raised, the best probably being 'Black Knight', 'Royal Red' and 'White Profusion'. Of the other Buddleia species, *B. alternifolia* has long arching sprays of lavender-blue flowers in summer, and *B. salvifolia* has creamy-white scented flower spikes up to 12cm in length, blooms in late summer and periodically throughout the rest of the year.

The genus is named after the Reverend Adam Buddle, Vicar of Farnbridge, Essex, and a keen amateur botanist. The connection between men of the cloth and botanical discoveries has been a constant theme in the history of plant collecting, as the achievements of Charles Plumier in the Americas and William Colenso in New Zealand testify. It would be too facile to suggest that they did not busy themselves enough with their parishes; rather they found God's creation endlessly fascinating.

CULTIVATION

Buddleia davidii could not be easier to cultivate, although it takes a little care to make it give of its best. A good fertile soil in a sunny position suits it the best. Regular watering is important, especially during hot weather, and a complete fertilizer should be applied in spring. It flowers on the growths made in the current season, so it should be pruned back to within two buds of the old wood after flowering. Cuttings strike readily if taken from short side-shoots, with a heel, in late summer and autumn and put in a cold frame. *B. davidii* is deciduous in cold districts and evergreen where warmer. The species is susceptible to caterpillars.

FEATURES

Height: 3m
Flowering period: Summer
Colour: Mauve
Scent: Very sweet

1 Sepal
2 Ovary
3 Stigma
4 Stamen

CALLISTEMON CITRINUS

Red Bottlebrush; Lemon Bottlebrush; Endeavour Bottlebrush

*I*N 1768, Joseph Banks set out with Captain Cook on the *Endeavour* to Tahiti and then on to find out more about the southern land which Tasman had glimpsed so tantalizingly in 1642. After landing in New Zealand, they eventually found Australia, dropping anchor at Botany Bay, on the south coast, in April 1770. With his companion, Dr Daniel Solander, Banks did much good botanizing there before the *Endeavour* sailed north to the Barrier Reef. Among the specimens pressed were species of *Callistemon*. The Endeavour Bottlebrush, *C. citrinus,* is a beautiful bushy, evergreen shrub which has a magnificent display of bright red flowers, tipped with yellow, in spring and periodically throughout autumn. The flower spikes grow to about 10cm in length, and the plant has tough, lance-like, dull green leaves. Other popular species in this native Australian genus include *C. linearis,* the Narrow-Leaved Bottlebrush; *C. salignus,* the White Bottlebrush, which has white flower spikes; and *C. viminalis,* the Weeping Bottlebrush, which has red flowers that appear in spring, summer and sometimes winter.

CULTIVATION

These hardy and extremely adaptable natives are suited to a wide variety of soil conditions and climates except for the coldest regions. They are also tolerant of salt, which makes them ideal shrubs for seaside gardens. *C. citrinus* does best in ordinary soil in full sunlight or partial shade and although able to survive dry conditions responds best to regular weekly soakings. It should be fed in spring with a slow-release fertilizer specially prepared for native plants or with a blood and bone mixture. Care should be taken not to disturb the plant's roots, and a mulch made from grass cuttings or manure helps keep down weeds while retaining soil moisture. Annual pruning after flowering helps to encourage good flower development in the following season. Propagation is from cuttings taken in spring and summer or from seeds gathered from the parent plant and sown in sheltered and moist trays in spring. The trays should be kept from direct sunlight until the seeds germinate, and after the seedlings have developed one or two pairs of leaves they can be transferred to pots and eventually, when the root system is sufficiently grown, to the garden. Sawflies and caterpillars may damage the leaves.

FEATURES

Height: Up to 3m
Flowering period: Spring and autumn
Colour: Crimson or bright red

1 Petal
2 Ovary
3 Stigma
4 Stamen

CAMELLIA JAPONICA

*C*AMELLIA JAPONICA is a native of Japan, although it has also been cultivated in China for centuries. It was named after the Moravian Jesuit George Joseph Kamel who travelled in Asia during the 17th century. In 1738, Lord Petre acquired from the East two plants, one single white, the other single red. Grown in a hothouse in England, these soon died. Fortunately, Petre's gardener had propagated one of them and grew it successfully in a coolhouse in the nursery he opened in the Mile End Road in 1740. Double forms arrived from Asia in later years.

By the 1840s, *C. japonica* was very popular and modish in Europe. "La Dame aux Camellias", Marie Duplessis, who died in 1852, aged 28, always wore camellias, but although she was the most famous person to do so she was only one among many.

C. japonica became very popular during the Victorian era, spreading throughout Europe, America and the Antipodes. Despite a period when it fell from favour in the late 19th century — it was considered too formal and had no scent — *C. japonica* has since enjoyed a revival and is perhaps the most popular species of this easily grown and long-lived evergreen shrub.

C. japonica has leaves that are very dark green and glossy, and oval with shallow toothing. The flowers, which are often semi-double, can be pink, white or red, and are up to 12cm across. Some varieties have striped or mottled flowers.

CULTIVATION

Camellias enjoy similar growing conditions to azaleas and rhododendrons, favouring semi-shady locations, near a building or underneath a large tree in soil that is filled with plenty of organic matter and not too limy. They must be kept moist but not allowed to become waterlogged so good drainage and a mulch of grass cuttings to retain moisture is essential. Weekly soakings are preferred to regular light watering. In extremely hot areas camellias are best grown in shadehouses to prevent sunlight from scorching the flowers. Frost can also be a problem in cold areas. *C. japonica* requires little or no pruning, unless there are inconvenient shoots on wall specimens; these can be cut off in spring. Weak or dead wood should also be removed. Pests include birds, which damage flower buds, red spider mites, bud mites, scale insects and caterpillars.

Camellias are relatively difficult to propagate and growth is slow for the first four or five years. Propagation is by cuttings taken in early summer or by seeds, which are best gathered from semi-double or informal double blooms. Seeds are most commonly germinated in a glass jar filled with sterilized peat moss and later transferred to a pot containing peat moss, sand and potting compost. *C. japonica* is grown in shrubberies, as hedges or in pots and tubs. Plants should be fed with complete fertilizer twice a year, using potash in autumn to encourage flower development and blood and bone mixture in spring to promote spring growth.

FEATURES

Height: Up to 5m
Flowering period: Winter and early spring
Colour: White, pink or red

1 Petal
2 Stigma
3 Stamen
4 Ovary

1 2 3 4

CHAENOMELES SPECIOSA

Flowering quince; Japonica

*C*HAENOMELES SPECIOSA is one of many good plants introduced to Britain by Sir Joseph Banks — or, in this case, sent home to Banks from China by James Main in 1796. It has been called both *Cydonia* and *Pyrus* in the past but has now settled down as *Chaenomeles*. The generic name comes from the Greek works *chaino,* meaning "I gape", and *meles,* "apple", although it is hard to see why or how it received this name.

It is a deciduous shrub which, if left alone, will make a broad shape. It has spiny branches and the serrated leaves are oval and quite glossy above. The flowers, which can be as much as 4.5cm across, are produced in clusters on last year's "wood". Small saucer-shaped blooms, ranging from bright red to pink, white, orange or apricot, appear in mid-winter for up to six weeks, making a welcome sight against bare branches. The fruit, which has no stalk, has small dots all over it' and smells like the quince, to which the plant is plainly closely related, but it remains green and is not as decorative as the golden fruit of *C. japonica*. The fruit is edible but has an unpleasant taste.

There are some very good varieties of *C. speciosa*. Among the best are 'Rubra Grandiflora', which has large crimson flowers and 'Nivalis', which has pure white flowers. *C. speciosa* is a parent of many hybrids which have arisen between it and the later-flowering *C. japonica*. These are called, collectively, *C × superba*.

CULTIVATION

Chaenomeles are easy to grow, requiring only a sunny place in any ordinary moist garden soil to flourish. Regular watering is beneficial in dry weather. If the soil is very alkaline, a dressing of peat each year will probably prevent yellowing of the leaves. A complete fertilizer or a blood and bone mixture should be applied in spring. Birds can attack the flowers; if this happens, some form of netting should be laid over them as protection. *Chaenomeles* require little or no pruning but the plant can be kept tidy if it is cut back after flowering. Cuttings of semi-hard wood can be taken in late summer and struck in a propagating case which has bottom heat. Long shoots can be layered.

FEATURES

Height: 2m
Flowering period: Winter
Colour: White, pink, red, apricot or crimson, depending on variety
Scent: The fruits smell like true quinces

1 Petal
2 Stigma
3 Stamen
4 Ovary

CLEMATIS ALPINA

(ATRAGENE ALPINA)

*C*LEMATIS ALPINA is native to Central and Northern Europe as well as Northern Asia. Very occasionally, the synonym *Atragene alpina* is used because *C. alpina* belongs to the Atragene group — those clematis with flowers which have, between the pepals and stamens, a ring of petal-like structures called petaloid staminodes. Clematis do not have petals — or, at least, not obvious ones: instead, the flowers are made up of four oval sepals. The staminodes of flowers of the Atragene group can make them look double.

C. alpina is a deciduous climber, with leaves up to 15cm long; these have nine leaflets which are dark green, narrowly oval, and deeply toothed. The flowers, which are violet-blue, are borne in spring on long stalks and they nod. The four sepals are 4cm long, the grey staminodes much less. This is not a strong-growing clematis, in comparison with many other species, so it is seen to its best advantage scrambling through a shrub or over a tree stump. More popular are *C. montana,* which has pale pink spring flowers, and *C.* × *jackmanii,* which has violet purple summer flowers. Many varieties are available including 'Nellie Moser', 'Superba' and 'Star of India'.

CULTIVATION

Clematis are twining plants, which means that they naturally clamber over trees and shrubs — hence their need to have their roots in shade. The traditional way of ensuring this is to plant low-growing evergreen shrubs around their bases or to place flat stones or tiles on the ground around the bases. All *Clematis* are like a deep, well-drained fertile soil and are, contrary to popular belief, not fussy whether it contains lime or not. They should be located in filtered light and given a spring mulch of rotted manure, peat or compost. No clematis likes being disturbed. *C. alpina* needs pruning only when grown in a place where its natural growth may prove a nuisance. If this is the case, prune out the flowered shoots after flowering.

Propagation of clematis is from semi-hardwood cuttings taken in summer or from hardwood cuttings taken in winter. They can also be raised from seed sown in autumn. Aphids, slugs and earwigs may damage the plant.

FEATURES

Height: Up to 2.4m
Flowering period: Spring
Colour: Violet-blue

1 Sepal
2 Ovary
3 Stamen
4 Petal

CYCLAMEN PERSICUM

Florist's Cyclamen

*C*YCLAMEN PERSICUM is of Mediterranean origin and was probably introduced to Britain from Cyprus in 1731. The Greek word *cyclos* (or *kyklos*) means "circle"; the plant's generic name may refer to the shape of the seedpod, or the spiral the stalk makes as the seedpod matures, or even the rounded tuber.

C. persicum has fragrant pink flowers which appear in winter and spring. The leaves are dark green, mainly heart-shaped, and have characteristic "marbling" or "silvering" on them. The flower-stem of this particular species does not spiral as the fruit matures. Other varieties have white, red and mauve flowers.

CULTIVATION

C. persicum should be planted in a very well drained soil enriched with organic matter, such as charcoal, in a warm but not sunny corner where it can be protected by shrubs. The corms cannot be divided so freshly dug-up seeding corms should be planted about 2.5cm deep in spring or early summer. These are more likely to retain some roots, making it easier to identify which is the bottom and which the top of the corm — never an easy matter. Alternatively, pot-grown corms can be bought from some nurseries, which solves that particular problem. Corms more than three years old are best replaced with new plants that have been grown from seed. *C. persicum* can also be grown in pots containing loam, leafmould, peat and sand in equal parts and kept indoors in a well-ventilated, well-lit and protected spot that receives two or three hours of sun each day.

Seed of *C. persicum* and of modern greenhouse varieties is sown in late summer or early autumn in a seed box filled with a mixture of garden loam, sand and peat moss. The mixture should be moist (stand the box in water until moisture has reached the surface) and the seeds planted 2 to 3 cm apart to a depth of 6mm. When the seedlings appear they should be pricked out into larger pots. The pots need to be regularly watered but not overwatered. Buds appear in autumn, and the plant should receive regular feeds with liquid fertilizer until flowering ends in late spring. *C. persicum* is susceptible to fungal disease.

FEATURES

Height: 20cm
Flowering period: Winter and spring
Colour: Pink
Scent: Yes

1 Petal
2 Ovary
3 Stigma

1 *2* *3*

DAHLIA COCCINEA

*T*HIS was one of the first dahlias to be introduced into Europe from their native Mexico. It went first to the Botanic Gardens at Madrid in 1789, and was named in honour of a Swedish pupil of Linnaeus called Dahl. In 1804, Lady Holland sent seed from Madrid to Mr Buonaiuti, her husband's Italian librarian in England, who grew it successfully. At the same time it was being cultivated in France, most notably in Empress Josephine's garden at Malmaison; some new cultivars found their way to Britain at the end of the Napoleonic Wars. By 1829 J.C. Loudon was reporting in his *Encyclopaedia of Gardening* that it was "the most fashionable flower in this country, and the extent of its cultivation in some of the nurseries..... is truly astonishing". Joseph Paxton wrote a book about its culture in 1838. The Dahlia became a florist's flower, grown, like the pinks, by the Paisley weavers. Dahlias were at the height of their popularity in the mid-19th century, after which there was a decline, when they were preserved primarily in cottage gardens. This century has seen a revival, and dahlias are a popular flower in Australian and New Zealand gardens. Unfortunately, in the process of development, a great deal of the charm of the original three species has been sacrificed for size and shape of flowerhead. Of the many cultivars presently in cultivation, it is thought that only the single-flowered ones have *D. coccinea* blood, the rest being primarily descendants of *D. pinnata* and *D. rosea*. The pure *D. coccinea* is grown only in botanical collections.

The colour range of the flowers of the species *D. coccinea* is from yellow through orange to bright red. The flowers are held on 90cm high stems, which often branch; the leaves are pinnate with narrowly ovate leaflets.

CULTIVATION

Dahlias are easy to grow, either from tubers or from seed. Tubers are lifted in winter when the plants have died back and stored until spring when they start to shoot. The tuber should be planted in 10 cm of soil with the shoot just below the surface. Seeds are sown in spring or summer in moist trays. Seedlings appear within two and four weeks and can be transplanted when they are 5 to 7cm tall. Dahlias do best in well-drained friable soil that has been prepared with organic material beforehand. Lime will improve acidy soils, while peat moss or leafmould is necessary to prepare sandy soils. *D. coccinea* needs regular watering during dry periods for the plant has large, thirsty leaves, and water-stress affects the flowering adversely. When the buds appear the plant can be fed with liquid fertilizer every fortnight to promote large flowers. Further bud formation can be achieved during flowering by removing spent blooms. The plants will also need to be staked. Stems should also be "stopped" to encourage branching, and dahlias grown for show are debudded regularly, so that there are only a few, but large, flowers. Pests and diseases include red spider mite, aphids and fungal diseases.

1 — Stem
2 — Tuber
3 — Root

1   Stem
2   Tuber
3   Root

FEATURES

Height: Up to 90cm
Flowering period: Late summer through autumn
Colour: Yellow, orange, red

DAPHNE ODORA

Sweet Daphne

*D*APHNES give a great deal of trouble to gardeners, yet we are always ready to cultivate them, even though they often do not thrive at all or suddenly die for no apparent reason. Their neat long-lasting flowers and, above all, their scent are enough to make all but the dullest gardener long to grow them. The most popular example of this genus in Australia is *D. odora,* a native of Japan and China which was introduced to the West in the late 18th century.

It makes a neat evergreen bush up to about 1.5m high in a well-favoured place. The leaves are oval and tapered at the base, up to 8cm long but quite narrow. They are dark green and shiny above, and paler below. The flowers are waxy and very fragrant, and are dark rose-pink in colour. They are produced in a cluster of about 10 flowers, each one 1cm across. These appear throughout late winter and continue during early spring.

There are three varieties of *D. odora* in cultivation. 'Rubra', the best known, has rose-pink flowers; 'Alba' has white flowers; and 'Variegate' has gold margined leaves with rose-pink flowers.

CULTIVATION

D. odora is best grown in partial shade (no more than half a day's sun) where it is well protected from hot summer winds and from bleak winter southerlies. It thrives in a loamy soil, fortified with leafmould, that is slightly acid and well drained. Although *D. odora* likes plenty of water during dry spells it languishes if allowed to become waterlogged. It should be fed in spring and summer with a mixture of blood and bone and well-matured leafmould. *D. odora* is susceptible to root-rot so it is important to avoid digging around the roots as this may facilitate the spread of the disease. Scale and virus diseases may also be a problem. Propagation is by soft tip cuttings taken in summer and placed in a free-draining peat and sand mixture in a cold frame. Once rooted they are potted up and eventually planted in the garden after they have reached a reasonable size. If there are low-growing shoots on the bush, these can be layered in early summer.

FEATURES

Height: 1—1.5m
Flowering period: Late winter and early spring
Colour: Rose-pink
Scent: Very scented

1 Petal
2 Stamen
3 Ovary

DIANTHUS PLUMARIUS

Garden Pink

*D*IANTHUS PLUMARIUS is the Pink, as opposed to the Carnation, and altogether a daintier and more useful garden plant. It is a native of the Alps, of Austria and of Hungary. In the 16th century Pinks were called "Feathered Gillofers" (gillyflowers) or "Soppes in Wine", this last because they were dipped in wine to impart a clove-like scent. Gerard grew them, and is supposed to have named them *plumarius* because of the "feathered" (deeply cut) petals. Parkinson had 17 varieties, and John Tradescant the Elder found them while on a trip to Russia in 1618. The first laced pink saw the light of day in 1772; it was called "Duchess of Lancaster" and was described as "laced" because the edges of its petals were tipped with the same colour as the central blotch. The laced pinks were much grown by the Paisley weavers (indefatigable searchers after new florists' flowers) in the mid-19th century, and also by north-country miners. The Paisley weavers were obsessed by pinks in the period between 1828 and 1850, and in that time they raised more than 300 sorts.

On the face of it there seems no connection between the word *Dianthus,* or even "gillyflower", and that of "carnation" — indeed, even when one does know the connection, it seems far-fetched. The Greeks, who called *D. caryophyllus* the "divine flower", made garlands (Latin *coronae*) of it, which is how it is supposed to have got the name "carnation". The specific epithet *caryophyllus* means "nut-leaved", and derives from the similarity between its scent and that of the clove (the "leaved" part refers to the leaves of the tree from which cloves are harvested). It all seems very insubstantial, but there it is.

The descendants of *D. plumarius* are both the "old-fashioned" pinks and the modern pinks. The plants have similar leaves to carnations but their flowers are much simpler. All have grey-green leaves and flowers up to 5cm across and stems up to 35cm high. Their flowers are strongly scented, and pinks make excellent edging or rockery plants.

CULTIVATION

Garden pinks repay care taken over their cultivation, although they will survive in an ordinary soil without much difficulty. They will languish in a waterlogged soil, however; so, if the drainage is suspect, the soil should be dug and raised and grit should be incorporated to lighten it. They are one of the groups of plants which genuinely grow better in an alkaline soil, so, if the soil is acid, a dressing of lime is advisable. They enjoy plenty of sun and are tolerant of dry conditions but will require some watering in times of drought. A potash feed in spring will aid flower development. Pinks (especially the "old-fashioned" varieties when newly planted) are rather loath to make good flowering side-shoots unless encouraged to do so, so early flowers should be snapped off. After they have flowered, a trim over and potash feed will encourage them to flower again.

Propagation is mainly by cuttings taken in mid-summer. Take side-shoots, about 7.5cm long and with plenty of sap, trim them off and put in a cuttings compost in a cold frame. They are easy to layer at the same time; this id done by cutting up from below a node to make a peg of stem and fixing the peg in contact with the soil using a piece of bent wire.

FEATURES

Height: Up to 35cm
Flowering period: Summer and autumn
Colour: Various; white or many shades of pink
Scent: Spicy

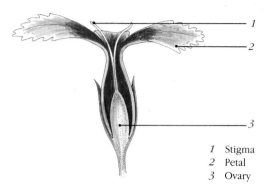

1 Stigma
2 Petal
3 Ovary

DIERAMA PULCHERRIMUM

Angel's Fishing Rods

*T*HIS is a very beautiful, graceful plant, far too rarely grown. It has tufted, grassy leaves, and thin arching stems 1.5m long at most, with pink or red pendulous trumpet-shaped flowers which appear in spring and summer. It was introduced to the West by the Backhouse of York nursery in 1865 from the Buffalo River region of eastern South Africa. There is a white form as well as several named cultivars, such as 'Windhover' (a very tall rose-pink variety) and 'Port Wine' (purple), mainly raised by W. Slinger and his son Leslie before the war at the famous, now defunct Slieve Donard nursery, in Northern Ireland. These days it is hard to find any *Dierama,* except the species, mentioned in nursery catalogues.

CULTIVATION

As *D. pucherrimum* is native to South Africa, one would expect the corms to be unreliably hardy. That is in fact the case, but, except in very cold localities, it is safe to leave them in the ground through the winter provided some sort of blanket protection can be given. In very cold places the corms should be lifted in late autumn and stored as one would *Dahlia* or *Acidanthera,* then replanted deeply in spring. Dieramas like a well-drained but fertile soil, enriched with leafmould or compost, and are happiest in full sun — although they will tolerate, and flower in, some shade. They can be increased by sowing seed in spring and planting out the seedlings in the autumn; or the corms can be lifted and divided in winter and the small offsets planted in a nursery row to grow on for a year before being planted where they are to flower. If possible, it is best to leave them in peace if they are to flower every year. They look especially attractive planted against a dark background which helps to highlight *D. pulcherrimum's* delicate flower colours.

FEATURES

Height: Up to 1.5m
Flowering period: Spring and summer
Colour: Pink

1 Ovary
2 Stamen
3 Petal
4 Style

DIGITALIS PURPUREA

Foxglove

A classic cottage garden species, *Digitalis purpurea* is native to Britain and has been used in the treatment of epilepsy for hundreds of years. The discovery of digitalin's usefulness for heart complaints, however, is of comparatively recent origin. Dr William Withering first used it in the control of dropsy at the end of the 18th century, but it was not until a little later that its efficacy as a heart stimulant was appreciated. It is one of the few native British plants used in modern medicine. The suffix "glove" is thought to stem from the Saxon word for "bell".

A biennial often grown as a border plant, *D. purpurea* is free-seeding and sometimes a nuisance, but its purple or white flowers (spotted inside the "glove") associate well with Old Roses, and it will flower (from the bottom of the stem upwards) throughout spring until the end of summer. In a good soil it will reach 1.5m in height. If it is desired that the plants be perennial, their seed-heads should be swiftly removed to prevent them wasting energy in seeding. Foxgloves feature large grey-green, oblong and crinkly leaves that grow as a rosette.

The species is the least attractive of the foxgloves, easily eclipsed by the 'Excelsior' strain, whose flowers are held so that the markings may be seen easily and whose colours range from white to cream, pink and purple. *D. ambigua* is a perennial with yellow brown flowers, which are intriguing, but the best is *D.×mertonensis,* a perennial with long-lasting strawberry-coloured tubular bells.

CULTIVATION

Cultivation of this plant is extremely easy; indeed, most people find that, within the confines of a tidy, orderly garden, its prodigal seeding makes its presence a decidedly mixed blessing. It is happiest in semi-shade and in ground which does not become too dry; it can survive in dry conditions but will not grow to its optimum height. It is very easily propagated by seed sown thinly outside in summer, and does best in soil that has been well mixed with compost. Although fairly hardy *D. purpurea* may be attacked by caterpillars and is prone to fungal disease.

FEATURES

Height: Up to 1.5m

Flowering period: Spring and summer

Colour: Purple or white, with dark spotting inside

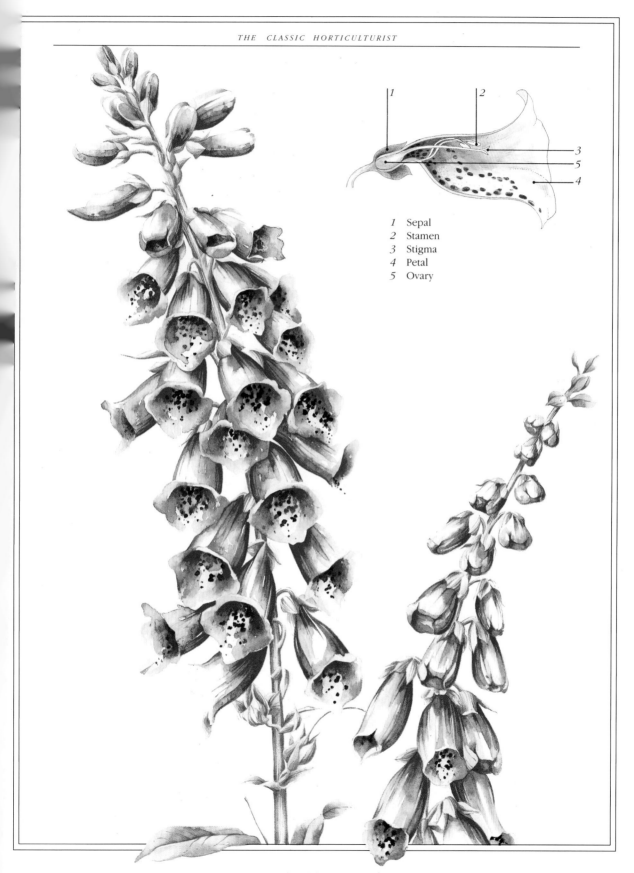

1 Sepal
2 Stamen
3 Stigma
4 Petal
5 Ovary

FRITILLARIA IMPERIALIS

Crown Imperial

*F*RITILLARIA IMPERIALIS, the Crown Imperial, is a native of Iran and of the Himalayas. It is one of those plants which, as a result of being cultivated for a very long time, has acquired accretions of legend and myth. There is an ancient Persian story that a wife wrongly accused of unfaithfulness was turned into this flower, and that she will continue to weep until such a time as she is united with her husband once more. Her "tears" are the nectaries which can be seen at the base of the flowers. E.A. Bowles recounts another story, that the Crown Imperial (which was then white) was growing in the Garden of Gethsemane and was too proud of its looks to bow its head when Jesus came. Since then, it has hung its head and blushed for shame with tears in its "eyes".

This plant was cultivated in Turkey for a long time before it was introduced to Vienna in 1576 by the botanist Clusius. It had certainly arrived in Britain by 1590. Gerard wrote of it:

> *This plant hath been brought from Constantinople, amongst other bulbous roots, and made denizons in our London gardens, whereof I have great plenty.*

It is a very noble plant, which has only one drawback — namely, that all parts of it smell strongly of fox. Apparently it used to be eaten in Persia, but only after being boiled until the evil smell (and poisonous properties) disappeared. Nevertheless, the Persians must have had strong stomachs! Bowles likened the smell to

> *a mixture of mangy fox, dirty dog-kennel, the small cats' house*

at the Zoo, and Exeter Railway Station, where for some unknown reason the trains let out their superfluous gas to poison the travellers. [*My Garden in Spring, 1914.*]

The plant will reach from 90cm to 1.5m tall in good conditions. It has lanceolate fleshy green leaves which are carried in what are called "whorls" to halfway up the thick, dark stems. The flowers, below a topknot of leaves, hang, are about 5cm long, and bloom in spring. They are usually orange in colour, although there are yellow or red varieties such as *F. maxima lutea* and *F. maxima rubra*. After the flower is fertilized, the seeds begin to form in a large fruit which gradually turns upwards.

CULTIVATION

Once planted, these bulbs are happiest left alone to flower, which they do for many years without degeneration. They prefer a position in full sun, except in very hot regions, but will tolerate a certain degree of dappled shade. *F. imperialis* needs plenty of water in spring and summer but should be left dry when the leaves turn yellow. The plant also needs protection from wind. The bulbs are very easily damaged by careless handling, and you are wise to wear gloves when planting them, as much to protect yourself from the smell as to protect the plant from harm. They should be planted between 10 and 12cm deep and 30cm apart in summer and, because they have hollow centres, they should be planted on their sides to prevent them from filling with water. Bulbs should be lifted in summer after

they have been left alone for three years. Snails can be a problem. *F. imperialis* is best planted in clumps or in a rockery.

FEATURES

Height: 90m–1.2m
Flowering period: Spring
Colour: Pale orange
Scent: Strong and unpleasant

1 Ovary
2 Nectar drops
3 Stamen
4 Stigma
5 Petal

FUCHSIA FULGENS

*F*UCHSIAS were discovered by the peripatetic French priest and botanist Charles Plumier during his travels through South America and the West Indies at the close of the 17th century. Plumier's specimen, which he named *Fuchsia triphylla coccinea* (this was before Linnaeus had shortened the Latin coding system), was picked up in San Domingo and featured four stamens. As more species of fuchsia were collected, each with eight stamens, botanists began to question Plumier's accuracy, suggesting that *F. triphylla coccinea* in fact belonged to an entirely separated genus. By 1877 Hemsley of Kew was publicly voicing his disbelief, claiming:

> *That the figure* [*illustration*]
> *is so rude that nobody, I believe,*
> *has been able to identify it with*
> *any living or dried plant.*
> *Possibly it is not a fuchsia at all*
> *in the sense of the present*
> *application of the name, for it is*
> *represented as having four*
> *stamens.*[21]

It was not until 1882 that a four-stamen fuchsia, developed in New York from seeds brought from the West Indies, was brought to Kew and Plumier vindicated. Another species, *F. coccinea,* arrived in England in the late 18th century and was brought for Kew by James Lee in 1788, quickly becoming a popular garden flower.

Since then the number of known fuchsia varieties has declined from an estimated 1,500 to about 500, although various fuchsia societies are having some success in reviving old favourites. The genus has numerous hybrids, and the tubular-shaped hanging flowers assume a wide variety of shape, size and colour. One of the most popular Australian species is the scarlet-flowered *F. fulgens,* the ancestor of many of today's most successful hybrids. *F. procumbens,* a New Zealand native with purple and yellow flowers, also thrives in antipodean gardens.

CULTIVATION

Despite their somewhat fragile appearance these evergreen shrubs are fairly hardy plants and thrive in well-drained and well-mulched soil in semi-shaded conditions. *F. fulgens* can be grown in garden beds, pots or hanging baskets and like other fuchsias can be propagated from soft tip cuttings in summer. It should be pruned sparingly in spring and is susceptible to attacks by red spider mites.

FEATURES

Height: Up to 1.5m
Flowering period: Summer and autumn
Colour: Scarlet

1 Ovary
2 Petal
3 Sepals
4 Style
5 Stamens

GALANTHUS NIVALIS

Common Snowdrop

*T*HE well-known Common Snowdrop, *Galanthus nivalis,* is indigenous to France and to Eastern Europe as far as the Caucasus. Some people believe it was introduced to Britain, where it grows naturally in single and double forms, from Italy by monks in the 15th century for use during the Feast of the Purification of the Virgin (or, as we better know it, Candlemas). During this festival, the image of the Virgin Mary would be removed from its usual resting-place and snowdrops put there in its stead. The snowdrop, therefore, became a symbol of purification. Gerard mentions it, calling it the "Early Flowering Bulbous Violet" (everything was a violet in those days — unless it was a lily!) The plant has a documented history much older than that, however, for in 300 BC Theophrastus mentioned that the snowdrop was growing on Mount Hymettus.

It grows in cool, moist regions throughout temperate south-eastern Australia and New Zealand. The flower stem grows to 25cm tall, although it can be much shorter, especially if the bulbs are crowded. The white, bell-shaped flower is about 2.5cm long; the inner segments are streaked with green. The flowers are faintly scented of honey. There are usually two leaves, which have a pronounced keel; they are linear and bluey-green in colour. Snowdrops are perfect for clump planting.

CULTIVATION

Snowdrops have the most agreeable trait of thriving best if left alone or if transplanted "in the green". This means that they are best moved just after flowering, when one can see them and when one thinks about it. Division is needed only when the clumps are *really* overcrowded. once you know this much about snowdrops there is little more you need to know. They grow anywhere, provided that the soil does not dry out, which means they are happy on heavy loams, well-mixed with decomposed compost, and they do not like the hot dry places which so many other good plants seem to require. Snowdrops should be watered during flowering. They like positions under deciduous trees where winter sun can penetrate and will grow in short grass. Propagation is by bulbs lifted in summer, separated and planted in autumn. Pests include snails and nematodes.

FEATURES

Height: 25cm
Flowering period: Winter and early spring
Colour: White with green streakings on inner petals
Scent: Faintly of honey

1 Ovary
2 Stamen
3 Stigma
4 Petal

GARRYA ELLIPTICA

The Silk Tassel Bush; Catkin Bush; Curtain Bush

*G*ARRYA ELLIPTICA is in its own family, Garraceae. It was found in 1828 by the famous British explorer and plant hunter David Douglas near the sea on the south side of the Columbia River in Oregon; it is also a native of California. It had actually been found some years before by Archibald Menzies, while on an expedition with Captain George Vancouver between 1790 and 1795, but it was not named by him. Douglas named it after the then deputy governor of the Hudson Bay Company, Nicholas Garry, as a mark of gratitude — the employees of the Hudson Bay Company were very helpful to him on his travels, providing him with guides and supplies. (Poor Douglas came to a sticky end in Hawaii in 1834, at the age of only 35, when he fell into a trap which already contained a wild bull. His introductions include many of our best-loved conifers, such as the Douglas fir, *Pseudotsuga taxifolia,* as well as the flowering currant, *Ribes sanguineum,* and the Oregon grape, *Mahonia aquifolium.*)

With *G. elliptica* the two sexes are on different plants. Each has different flowers. The male has grey-green catkins up to 16cm long and is considered to be the more garden worthy. The female flowers are more silvery in tone and up to 7.5cm in length. *G. elliptica* is an evergreen shrub, or occasionally small tree, with oval leaves which are green above and grey below. It flowers in summer and autumn. The fruits, which are produced only when there are male and female plants growing near to each other, are round, silky and a greenish-purple in colour, and appear in summer and autumn.

CULTIVATION

The most important thing to remember about the cultivation of garryas is that they do not like to be moved; most especially, they do not like their roots disturbed. They enjoy a sunny position, well protected from wind in loamy or sandy-loam soils. Plenty of organic matter should be mixed into the ground before planting. Garryas require a good soaking approximately once a week and do best in cold and cool temperate climates. A complete fertilizer needs to be applied in spring, and the plant should be pruned to shape after flowering. Propagation is from semi-hard wood cuttings, taken during summer or autumn and protected from the sun until they are well rooted. Thereafter they can be transferred to the garden. Garryas are fairly impervious to both pests and disease although severe frost will brown the tough leaves.

FEATURES

Height: 6m
Flowering period: Summer and autumn
Colour: Silver-grey

1 Petal
2 Stamen

HELLEBORUS NIGER

Christmas Rose

OVER the years, hellebores have attracted to themselves a wealth of superstition and story. This is hardly surprising when one-considers that they are poisonous (like so many of the Ranunculaceae) and yet, in small quantities, medicinally efficacious — for example, the alkaloids they contain have been used in the past as a drastic laxative and as a heart stimulant. The Greeks thought that hellebores could be used as a cure for madness, and this belief lingered on into the 17th century. Gerard, for example, reported that a 'purgation' of hellebore 'is good for mad and furious men, for melancholy, dull, and heavie persons, and briefly, for all those that are troubled with black choler and molested with melancholy'. To this end, the roots were dried, ground down, and taken like snuff. They were also thought to be useful for warding off evil spirits. The Christmas Rose even plays a part in a medieval mystery play. A country girl accompanying the shepherds cries because she has nothing, not even flowers, to bring to the Baby Jesus. An angel takes pity on her, touches the ground, and up flowers the Christmas Rose.

H. niger, being a *bona fide* cottage-garden plant, has enjoyed a good press from, for example, Gertrude Jekyll and Vita Sackville-West. The latter wrote:

> *I have a plant in my garden which to my certain knowledge has been there for fifty years. It was bequeathed to me by an old country-woman of the old type, who wanted me to have the enjoyment of it after she had gone.*

H. niger is so-called because its roots are very black. It comes from Central and Southern Europe, as well as western Asia. It is an evergreen perennial with dark green leathery leaves deeply divided into 7 or 9 segments. The veins on the leaves are very pronounced. The pure white saucer-shaped flowers, up to 7cm across and with yellow stamens, come out in succession during winter.

Other hellebores have flowers varying in colour from cream, pink and purple to green.

CULTIVATION

The Christmas Rose is one of the those plants about which gardeners are inclined to be wary, and rightly so. The reason is that it will thrive in some gardens but not in others, and there seems little rational explanation for why this should be so. The best hope of success lies in giving it a place in partial shade and in a soil which is rich and moist, but not waterlogged. Plants should be left sternly alone and not transplanted; the only attention they appreciate is a top-dressing of well-rotted compost or manure in summer; this acts also as a much needed mulch. The flowers can be cut in bud and brought inside where, if their stems are split, they will last quite well in water. If the plant must be divided, this should be done in early spring. Division is the usual way of increasing the plant, although it is possible to sow ripe seed in early summer in a seed tray which is placed

in a cold frame (hellebores are very hardy). Once germinated, the seedlings can be planted in a nursery bed until large enough to plant out.

FEATURES

Height: 45cm
Flowering period: Winter
Colour: White

1 Petal
2 Stamen
3 Stigma
4 Ovary

IRIS GERMANICA

Purple Flag; London Flag

*T*HE goddess Juno had a messenger, called Iris, whom she regularly sent down to Earth. Iris reached Earth by way of a rainbow bridge, and the Iris flower is named after her because it is found in such a rainbow of colours. *Iris germanica* was for long thought to be one of the parents of the modern garden Bearded iris hybrids but, in fact, these are primarily a mixture between *I. pallida* and *I. variegata*. However, *I. germanica* is the oldest cultivated European iris, having been grown at Lake Constance in the 9th century. It grows in the wild all over Europe and eastwards to India and Nepal. It is likely that it has been grown in gardens in the Middle East and the Mediterranean for centuries for its medicinal and cosmetic properties. In Italy, the rhizome was even used to make rosary beads. A subspecies is the famous *I. florentina;* this iris is the source of orris root, so popular in the Middle Ages and later, and was grown extensively around Florence for use in the preparation of beauty treatments and toothpastes. The roots of this iris, when fully dry, are very scented, which makes it ideal for perfuming toilet waters and for putting among household linen. The scent is similar to that given off by violets.

I. germanica and *I. florentina* are not the French Fleur-de-Lis. The honour for that must go to *I. pseudacorus,* the Yellow Flag Iris. The story goes that in the 6th century Clovis I, one of the Merovingian kings, was being pursued by the Goths near Cologne. He saw an iris growing in the middle of the Rhine and deduced rightly that the water must be sufficiently shallow for his men to cross in safety. He consequently adopted *I. pseudacorus* as his emblem. Six centuries later, Louis VII of France

copied him and wore the emblem while fighting in the Crusades, with the result that this iris acquired the common name Fleur-de-Louis, soon shortened to Fleur-de-Lis.

I. germanica grows up to 1.2m tall. It has greenish-blue leaves and scented flowers, the falls of which are purple, the beard yellow, and the standards mauve. It flowers in spring. *I. florentina* is a form of it; the flowers are white with a touch of blue on the falls.

CULTIVATION

Rhizomatous irises, like garden pinks, are happiest on a neutral or slightly alkaline soil. They like a soil into which well-rotted organic material and bonemeal have been incorporated and need to be watered frequently in the growing season. They are best planted soon after they have flowered. The rhizomes like to be "baked" by the sun in summer, so should be planted shallowly with the longest side facing the sun; they should not be shaded by other plants or weeds. In planting, their long "fans" of leaves should be cut back by half so that the plant does not lose too much water by transpiration before the roots are established. *I. germanica* needs to be dug up and divided every three years, to prevent the rhizomes becoming overcrowded and ceasing to flower freely. Division means throwing away the old central part of the rhizome and replanting only the younger branches; these can be divided by snapping them apart or using a sharp knife. The new transplants should be kept well watered until established, after which time watering will probably be unnecessary. A general balanced fertilizer sprinkled around the plants at planting time helps their development.

FEATURES

Height: Up to 1.2m
Flowering period: Spring
Colour: Bright purple with yellow
"beard"
Scent: Yes

1 Style
2 Stigma
3 Stamen
4 Ovary

JACARANDA MIMOSIFOLIA

*T*HIS handsome deciduous tree has spreading branches and clouds of lavender-blue flowers in late spring and early summer and is a native of South and Central America and the West Indies, where the genus numbers some 50 species. It was first introduced to the outside world in 1816 when Allan Cunningham, a plant hunter from Kew and protege of Sir Joseph Banks, brought a specimen of *Jacaranda ovalifolia* back from Brazil after a two-year collecting trip in company with fellow Kew man James Bowie. Cunningham went to Australia shortly afterwards, subsequently making his name as an explorer and botanist in several expeditions, including forays into the Blue Mountains, Illawarra district and the Bathurst-Mudgee region, before his death in 1839. He is commemorated by an obelisk in Sydney's Botanic Gardens, home to several jacarandas which were already attracting public attention in 1868 when the *Sydney Morning Herald* commented:

> *The jacaranda is perfectly hardy and although perhaps the most lovely and striking of all flowering trees, is but little known by reason of the great difficulty of propagation. This difficulty has, however, at last been solved by the well known firm of Messrs. Guilfoyle and Sons, Exotic Nursery, Double Bay. For this service alone the name of Guilfoyle deserves to be remembered.*

Of course William Guilfoyle, then leaving his father's employ for a collecting trip in the Pacific aboard the *Challenger,* later became world renowned as director of Melbourne's Botanic Gardens, where he made extensive use of jacarandas in his ambitious reorganisation of the work carried out by his predecessor Ferdinand von Mueller. Since then jacarandas have become a familiar sight in many parts of Australia, doing well in all climates except extreme tropical or very cold regions. Besides its beautiful display of bell-like blossoms, the jacaranda is distinguished by delicate fern-like leaves, which turn a golden-bronze in autumn, and graceful network of horizontal branches. The shape of the tree ranges from tall and narrow to broad and spreading, depending on the space available for growth.

CULTIVATION

J. mimosifolia has a deep and extensive root system and can survive in poor soils with as little as 650mm of rain annually. However, it prefers regular watering and rich soils and is best located in full sunlight. In colder regions it should be given protection from frost for three to four years until established. It should be fed annually with a slow-release fertilizer.

FEATURES

Height: 2.5m at five years; 12m at maturity
Flowering period: Late spring to early summer
Colour: Lavender-blue
Scent: None

1 Ovary
2 Style
3 Stamens
4 Stigma
5 Corolla

5
4
3
2
1

KNIPHOFIA GALPINII

Galpin's Red Hot Poker; Torch Lily

THIS is a dwarf Red Hot Poker, growing not more than 60cm tall, with stiff, narrow, grassy leaves and loose-flowered spikes which are orange but which fade a little as they age. It was introduced from southern Africa in 1930 and was immediately recognized as a good garden plant, because of its compact habit; it has since been the parent of several good garden cultivars. It was named after one Ernest Galpin, of Barberton, who had sought plants in South Africa in the 1890s. This species comes from the Transvaal, Swaziland and Natal. It is plainly very closely related to *K. macowanii* and *K. triangularis;* the *K. galpinii* of gardens may well be a subspecies of the latter. The work on hybridizing has been done by Amos Perry, Alan Bloom at Bressingham, the Slingers at Slieve Donard, and Beth Chatto. Among the best cultivars for gardens are 'Little Maid' and 'Sunningdale Yellow'.

Kniphofias, or *Tritoma* as they were called in the 19th century because many species have leaves with three edges to them, have always been popular border plants, even though the usual one seen, *K. uvaria,* is rather coarse and unsubtle in colour. In *The Wild Garden* (1870) William Robinson recommended that tritomas be planted in bold clumps, and Gertrude Jekyll grew them for their strong colour and imposing shape in September in her main flower border at Munstead Wood.

Other species and varieties include *K. praecox,* which flowers in late winter, and *K.* 'Ernest Mitchell', a citrus lemon-flavoured plant.

CULTIVATION

Kniphofias are amenable plants which need little or no feeding and desire only, like Greta Garbo, to be left alone. Being South African, however, they do not appreciate wet feet, and so are best planted in full sun and in a light, free-draining soil. In exposed or cold places some winter protection — straw, perhaps — is a help, especially when the plant is young. They should be planted in spring. The roots are fleshy and should not be allowed to dry out before planting. Red Hot Pokers do not need staking; they are quite capable of holding their heads up on their own. Propagation is done in spring, by division or by seed sown outside in rows.

FEATURES

Height: 1.2m
Flowering period: Summer
Colour: Flame and orange-yellow

1 Ovary
2 Stigma
3 Stamen
4 Petal

LILIUM CANDIDUM

Madonna Lily

*L*ILIUM CANDIDUM is the Madonna Lily. It is thought to be the oldest cultivated plant, although that is a theory very hard to prove — or disprove — conclusively. The Phoenicians knew of it, as did the Assyrians, and the Minoans of Crete painted it on their vases before 1600BC. It is likely that it was as much prized for its manifold medicinal qualities, which included cures for dropsy and for boils, as it was for its considerable beauty. The Roman army, for example, planted it near their permanent camps because of its supposed efficacy in curing corns, a condition from which such a mobile army must have suffered badly. It was probably the Romans who introduced it into Britain, perhaps from Salonika. It finds a place in Ion Gardener's early-15-century *The Feate of Gardening.*

It is a hardy lily which grows up to 1.5m in height. The flowers, several to a stem and the purest white except for the yellow pollen, are trumpet-shaped, with the petals reflexed at the ends. They are 9cm long and very, very fragrant. They flower in early summer. Other popular trumpet lilies include *L. regale,* the Regal Lily, which has white flowers with a yellow centre; and *L. longiflorum,* the Christmas Lily, which has white blooms.

CULTIVATION

L. candidum is not the easiest lily to grow, mainly because it is a martyr to *Botrytis* as well as lily virus. The first can be minimized by planting the lilies in a sunny place and spraying with Bordeaux mixture in warm, wet seasons. The second, which manifests itself as mottling and streaking on the leaves, requires that the infected bulb be dug up and burned to prevent its spread to other bulbs.

The bulbs should be planted shallowly, preferably in a slightly alkaline soil, with the top of the bulb just below soil level, as soon after the stem dies in autumn as possible, and thereafter left undisturbed. The soil should be enriched and, if it is heavy, lightened by digging in grit. As *L. candidum* is a species, its seeds will breed true and can be sown deeply in pots in early autumn. Growing from seed is also an advantage because this method helps prevent the spread of serious virus diseases. If growing from bulbs, buy young healthy-looking ones with closely packed scales and in good root system.

FEATURES

Height: 1.5m
Flowering period: Early summer
Colour: Pure white
Scent: Very strong and sweet

1   Stigma
2   Stamen
3   Ovary
4   Petal

MAGNOLIA × SOULANGIANA

Saucer Magnolia

MAGNOLIAS are the aristocrats of the garden; their lineage is ancient and their appearance most distinguished. Their line stretches back into the distant mists of time. It has been proved that they grew 5 million years ago which makes them as old as even the Maidenhair tree.

Magnolia × *soulangiana* is a hybrid between *M. denudata* and *M. liliiflora*. This cross took place by chance in the garden of the château belonging to M. Soulange-Bodin at Fromont outside Paris. M. Soulange-Bodin was the founder of the National Horticultural Society of France, so plainly he was a dedicated and knowledgeable gardener. Of this magnolia's parents, *M. liliiflora* is a Chines plant which was in fact introduced to Europe from Japan in 1790, and *M. denudata* is another Chinese magnolia which came in the year before and which is more usually known by its common name of Yulan. The result of the cross first flowered in 1826. There are now many forms of *M.* × *soulangiana* ranging from completely white to claret-purple in flower colour.

The honour of having his name perpetuated in this glorious genus went to Pierre Magnol. He was a botanist in Montpellier in France who never gained promotion while he was a Protestant. However, in 1694, he converted to Catholicism and this opened the way to his preferment, not only as a professor but also as Director of the Montpellier Botanic Gardens. In those days, religious divergence from state orthodoxy was a recipe for professional suicide.

M. × *soulangiana* makes a large spreading shrub. It is deciduous and has green leaves, up to 20cm long and tapering towards the apex; they are narrowly ovate or lanceolate, shiny above and downly below. The flowers, which appear in spring before the tardy leaves, are large and upright at first, later opening out as they mature. They are white but have pink staining at the base. The shrub continues to flower, although less impressively, even after the leaves have developed. One of the best varieties is called 'Lennei'. This originated in Italy but in 1854 was brought to Germany by a nurseryman who called it after Herr Lenné, the man in charge of the Royal Gardens in Berlin. It has rosy-purple flowers.

CULTIVATION

M. × *soulangiana* is quite the easiest of a difficult but very beautiful genus to grow, which is why it is so widely planted. For one thing, there is little doubt of its hardiness, and, for another, it will grow in any ordinary soil which is not too shallow. It does best in a sunny position with acid soil that has been well prepared with a mixture of manure or compost. If its preferences can be met it will grow reasonably swiftly, flower quickly (for a magnolia), and not be an anxiety or trouble as far as pests or diseases are concerned. It does respond positively to a mulch of well-rotted compost in spring, and the soil should not be allow to dry out.

Propagation by seed takes a long time and is anyway uncertain as this magnolia is a hybrid. Layering in spring is preferable. Cuttings can be taken in summer. Magnolias should not be pruned if it can be avoided.

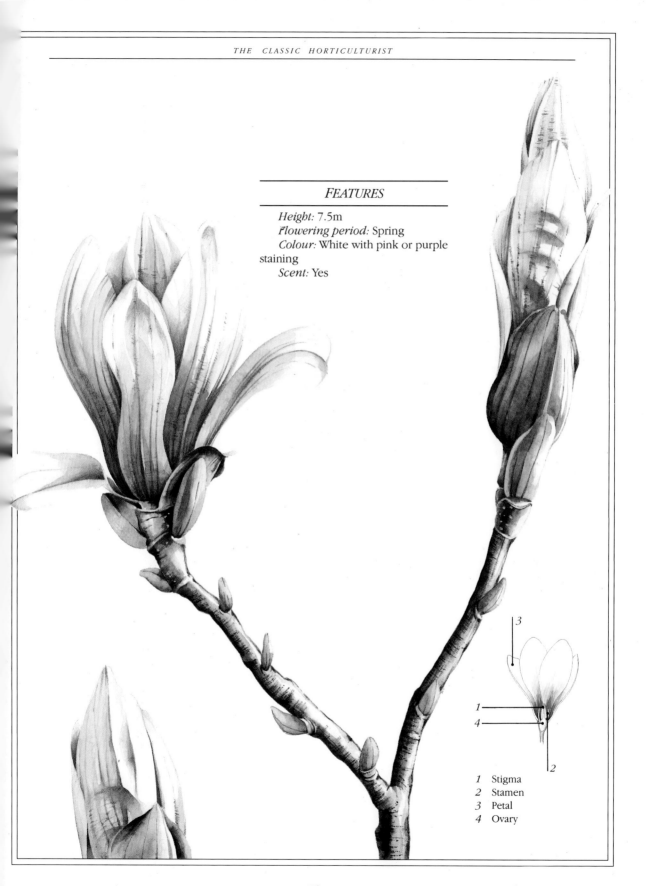

FEATURES

Height: 7.5m
Flowering period: Spring
Colour: White with pink or purple staining
Scent: Yes

1 Stigma
2 Stamen
3 Petal
4 Ovary

METROSIDEROS EXCELSA

Pohutukawa; New Zealand Christmas Tree

*T*HIS large New Zealand native evergreen features prominently in Maori mythology. Early migration legends tell how the first Polynesian migrants to Aotearoa (New Zealand) saw *Metrosideros excelsa's* spectacular red blossoms while still out to sea, later christening this coast-loving and salt-resistant species pohutukawa, which means "spray sprinkled". The pohutukawa is also associated with death. A massive specimen that grew at Cape Reinga, New Zealand's most northerly point, was believed to be the place of departure for spirits entering Reinga, the Maori underworld. Known as Aka of Reinga, this tree sent a branch far out over the water to which exiting souls clung before taking their final plunge into the hereafter. This branch was said to have broken off during the 1820s when incessant intertribal warfare produced such bloodshed that it was unable to support the weight of departing warriors. When the great New Zealand plant hunter Thomas Cheeseman visited the site in 1895 he found only a whitened stump.

Famed for its hard, durable wood and sometimes used for boat building and furniture making, *M. excelsa* thrives in warm frost-free coastal locations such as the northern part of New Zealand's North Island or the temperate shores of Australia. Besides being adapted to salt conditions it is also remarkably impervious to city pollution. The pohutukawa produces masses of scarlet flowers with gold-tipped stamens in dense clusters resembling bottlebrush spikes in late spring and early summer, hence its colonial name, the New Zealand Christmas Tree. It has rounded dark-green leaves with velvety silver-white undersurfaces, dark woody bark which often produces masses of brown or orange aerial roots (which, as they never anchor the tree to the ground, apparently serve no function) and a twisting root system that digs deep into the ground, sometimes enabling the tree to thrive in seemingly impossible locations such as cliff faces. *M. excelsa* 'Aurea' has pale yellow flowers.

CULTIVATION

M. excelsa can be grown in a pot from cuttings taken in late autumn or winter and transported to fertile well-drained and well-composted soil at any time of the year. It is generally resistant to pests and diseases and should be fed with a slow-release fertilizer specially formulated for native plants or a small amount of blood and bone in spring. Suitable as a free-standing tree or as a hedge, *M. excelsa* should be pruned after flowering to maintain shape and protected from frost for the first three years in colder regions.

FEATURES

Height: 3m at 10 years; 8m at maturity
Flowering period: Late spring to early summer
Colour: Scarlet

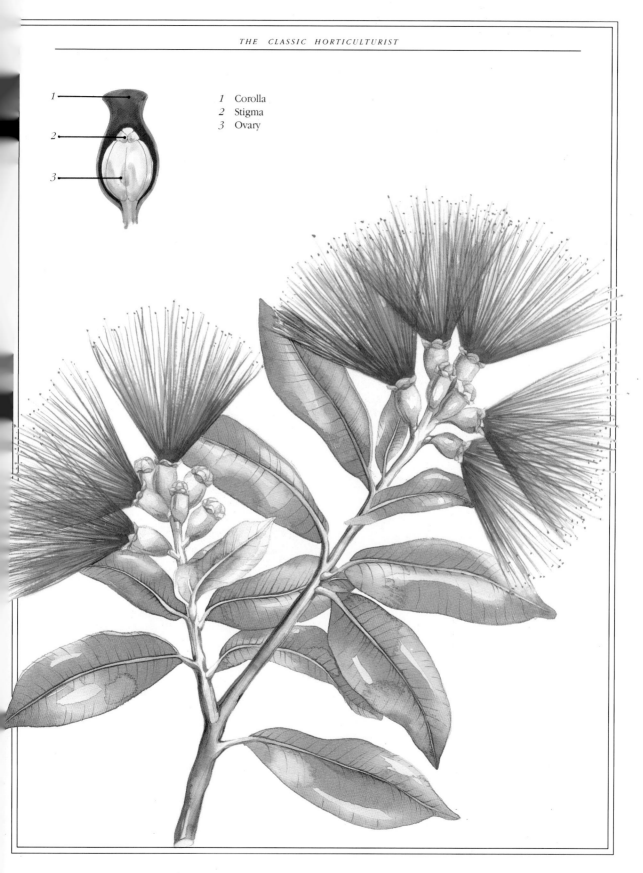

1   Corolla
2   Stigma
3   Ovary

MYOSITIS ALPESTRIS

Forget-Me Not

ALTHOUGH it seems cruel to dispel the layman's romantic notions, the experts could cast doubt on the identification of *Myosotis* as the original Forget-Me-Not. Some say the honour should properly go to the Germander speedwell. It may be that, in the past, one plant was meant by the name Forget-Me-Not in Britain and another by *Vergiss-Mein-Nich* in Germany. The most that can be said is that *Myosotis* seems now to have stabilized as *the* Forget-Me-Not and, that being the case, we might as well assume that it was always so. Henry Bolingbroke, later Henry IV, took the Forget-Me-Not (whatever it was) as his emblem, and the "S" (for *Souveignez* or *Souveraine*) came to be worn by those with Lancastrian allegiances as a sign or badge of their affiliation.

M. alpestris, although a native of Western Europe, was not grown as a garden flower until the 19th century. It was not until the 1870s that it became an important constituent of spring bedding schemes, associating particularly well with garden tulips. It has been the parent of many hybrids used for this purpose, notably 'Carmine King', 'Royal Blue', 'Blue Ball', and 'Alba'. The type plant has hairy stems and oblong-lanceolate leaves (which gives point to the name *Myosotis,* or "mouse-ears"), and delicious azure blue flowers with contrasting yellow eyes. It does not grow above 22cm tall, which is why is has always proved so useful as an edger to borders, but which rather undermines its effect when combined with tall tulips.

CULTIVATION

M. alpestris could not be easier to cultivate. Indeed, there are some who say it is too easy and takes liberties, spilling its seed with cheerful abandon all over tidy flower beds. Although liable to become a perennial if left alone *M. alpestris* is usually grown as an annual and is planted out in summer, thriving in a moist, semi-shaded position, preferably one that receives several hours of morning sun. A rich alkaline sandy loam is the best soil for Forget-Me-Nots, which appreciate regular watering. They are troubled by snails and caterpillars.

FEATURES

Height: 22cm
Flowering period: Spring
Colour: Azure blue with yellow eye
Scent: Yes

1 Stigma
2 Stamen
3 Petal

MYRTUS COMMUNIS

Greek Myrtle

*T*HERE is a great deal of folklore and tradition attached to the Myrtle. It was very important, for instance, in Roman mythology and the Romans may well have introduced it into Britain when they colonized the country in the 1st century AD. It is a plant which originally comes from the western part of Asia — Iran and Afghanistan — and was introduced to European gardens in the 16th century. The Roman goddess of love, Venus, wore a crown of it when she rose from the sea, and this connection with love has led to the tradition whereby Myrtle is included in a bride's wedding bouquet. By the 1770s there were at least 19 varieties grown in Britain and it was important as a cut flower. It was often grown outside in summertime in a tub and brought back under glass for the winter.

Myrtle is an evergreen shrub with very fragrant white flowers and leaves which are scented if crushed. The berries are black and round, and were certainly used by the Romans in cooking. The leaves are ovate and pointed, up to 5cm long, very dark green and shiny above but paler underneath. The flowers grow singly, on stalks; they arise from the axils in the leaves and have many prominent stamens. They come out in summer and make a good informal hedge. There is a double form and also a variegated-leaved myrtle called 'Variegata' which features an explosion of leaves with contrasting creamy-white edges.

CULTIVATION

M. communis may be grown in any good loamy soil as long as the location is well drained. The shrub responds well to both partial shade and full sun. Propagation is from seed or, most easily, from hardwood cuttings taken in summer and struck in sandy moist soil. It does best in temperate and mountain districts.

FEATURES

Height: 3—4m
Flowering period: Summer
Colour: White
Scent: Both flowers and foliage are aromatic

1 Stamen
2 Stigma
3 Petal

NARCISSUS PSEUDONARCISSUS
Lent Lily; Wild Daffodil

THERE are over 8,000 varieties of narcissus, divided into 11 divisions based on flower shape and colour. *N. pseudonarcissus* is a native of Britain. It was originally thought that only the short-trumpeted flowers of *Narcissus poeticus* were real daffodils, or 'affodyls' (a name also given to the white asphodel) — hence the specific name *pseudonarcissus*. Turner writes about it, as does Gerard, who reports it growing in London gardens 'in great abundance':

> *The flower groweth at the top, of a yellowish-white colour with a yellow crown or circle in the middle and flowereth in the month of April or sometimes sooner.*

N. pseudonarcissus has long, glaucous leaves and a drooping, trumpet-like corona of inner petals as long as, bur darker in colour than, the spreading perianth petals. It flowers in spring.

The Lent Lily has had something to do with the breeding of all the long-trumpeted garden daffodils. Among its most famous offspring are 'Golden Harvest', 'Queen of Bicolors', and 'Monk Hood'.

CULTIVATION

This plant and its garden hybrid descendants are most commonly grown in drifts amongst grass or among shrubs in borders. Indeed, they will grow anywhere with no fuss, provided they are left alone until the leaves start to yellow and die down. They do best when planted in organically enriched soil which does not dry out, because they may not flower the next year if they do not get enough moisture in the spring after flowering. Plant in full sun in cool areas and semi shade in hot districts. A hot, dry, sandy soil will impede the bulb's growth. They should be planted early in the autumn, immediately after they are received, so that they have time to make their roots before the winter. In grass this will require the use of a special "bulb planter" or a spade to lift the turf. They should be planted very deeply in cultivated borders in case they are damaged by forking, and at three times the depth of the bulb in grass.

Most people leave the bulbs alone for many years, especially those grown in grass. Those grown in borders will become congested earlier and will benefit from being lifted and divided every few years. This should be done in summer. Sowing by seed should be avoided: it is painfully slow and the results are unimpressive.

Narcissi are victims of various virus diseases. If mottling, streaking, or serrating of the leaf-edges is evident, the affected bulbs should be dug up and burned. This seemingly harsh measure is the only way of containing the virus.

FEATURES

Height: 20—36cm
Flowering period: Spring
Colour: Pale yellow
Scent: Yes

1 Petal
2 Stigma
3 Stamen
4 Ovary
5 Spathe

NICOTIANA ALATA (N. AFFINIS)

Tobacco Plant

*T*HIS is the ornamental Tobacco Plant, and should not be confused with the tobacco plant of commerce, which is *Nicotiana tabacum.* The genus was named after the French Ambassador to Portugal, Jean Nicot, who planted tobacco in the embassy garden in Lisbon in 1560 and introduced it to France. Sir Walter Raleigh brought it to Britain in 1585. The ornamental tobacco plant, *N. alata* var. *grandiflora,* comes from southern Brazil, where the leaves are smoked and chewed by the natives.

The advantage of the ornamental type, from the decorative point of view, over other types of tobacco plant is that it has less expanse of leaf. It usually grows to about 1m high, and all parts are sticky. The lower leaves are ovate and about 15cm long; the higher ones on the stem are a little smaller. The flowers of the species, which are borne on loose racemes, are 7.5cm long, greenish-yellow, and very fragrant at night. Modern varieties have been bred with flowers coloured from crimson through pink to white and green which will stay open during the daytime. Examples include 'Sensation Mixed' and 'Lime Green'.

CULTIVATION

N. alata is not difficult to grow, as long as it is appreciated that it is a half-hardy annual and requires to be sown in heat in late winter, pricked out into trays, hardened off, and planted out when there is no longer any danger of frost. The planting position should be in light shade and in a fertile, well drained soil. The modern varieties which remain open during the day are more ornamental; they are compact enough not to require staking. The Tobacco Plant suffers only from aphids, against which it is possible to spray.

FEATURES

Height: Up to 1m
Flowering period: Spring to summer
Colour: Greenish yellow
Scent: Very scented at night

1 Stigma
2 Petal
3 Stamen

PAEONIA OFFICINALIS

European Peony

*L*IKE many of our best-loved plants, Paeony (or Peony) was known to the Ancient Greeks and consequently has a mythological name. It was called after Paeon, a physician who used its roots to cure Pluto when he had been injured by Hercules. As with the Mandrake, it was thought that great care had to be taken to avoid pulling up the roots but, by the time Gerard was writing, this tradition was regarded as a "vaine and frivolous" superstition, "for the roote of Peionie, as also the Mandrake, may be removed at any time of the yeere, day or hower whatsoever". Good old Gerard, striking a blow for modern rationalism! Despite these brave words, however, it would be surprising if he had never fallen prey to superstitions just as "vaine and frivolous".

The genus originates in China, where 2,000 years ago it was known as "the king of flowers", and *P. officinalis* came to the West from the Mediterranean region before the middle of the 16th century. Within 20 years, according to William Turner, it had become common everywhere. By 1629, Parkinson was growing the two double varieties as well. (The double red, especially, is still widely cultivated in cottage gardens, despite the gorgeousness of the modern cultivars.) At that time the roots were thought to help in the treatment of epilepsy, and so unfortunate children had them hung around their necks.

This plant grows up to 60cm tall. The leaves, which colour interestingly in autumn, are deeply cut into segments, these segments being as much as 10cm long. The flowers of the type species are blood-red, bowl-shaped, and produced in spring.

P. lactiflora, another herbaceous perennial, features white, purple, red or pink poppy-like flowers in single, semi-double or double varieties in spring and is the most popular species grown in Australasia.

CULTIVATION

Paeonies cause consternation, they have an infuriating habit of not flowering for several years after they have been planted. This will not happen, however, if it is appreciated that the crown with the buds must be no more than about 2.5cm below the surface of the soil. Generally speaking, it is fair to say that paeonies prefer to be left where they are and not moved about regularly; indeed, they have been known to inhabit the same spot happily for half a century or more in Europe.

Paeonies like a well dug fertile soil, and water in dry weather; they also enjoy an annual spring mulch. They will almost certainly lean if not staked, especially if rain falls on the heavy flower-heads of the double forms. They *can* be divided, if necessary, in autumn, and the species may be grown from seed, sown in that month and put in a cold frame. They can suffer from leaf spot damage and also paeony wilt.

FEATURES

Height: 60cm
Flowering period: Spring
Colour: Red

1 Petal
2 Stamen
3 Stigma
4 Ovary

PHILADELPHUS CORONARIUS

Sweet Mock Orange

*T*HERE is an interesting history attached to the Philadelphus. It was introduced to Europe by the Holy Roman Emperor's Ambassador to the Court of Suleiman the Magnificent, Ogier Ghiselin de Busbecq, who brought it back with him on his return to Vienna in 1562. He also brought with him the Common Lilac (*Syringa vulgaris*) at the same time, and the names became confused. That is why, even today, *Philadelphus* is often called *Syringa,* properly the Latin name for Lilac. The wood of both these plants is pithy in the middle, so stems could be made into pipes; consequently these plants were originally called the White Pipe and the Blew Pipe trees.

Philadelphus had arrived in Britain before 1597. Gerard mentions in that year that he has it flowering in his garden. Curiously, he did not care for the fragrance which we find so delicious – indeed, he relates that when flowers were put in his room the smell woke him up and so he "cast them out of my chamber".

Philadelphus means "brotherly love"; the reason for the name is unclear. The common name, Sweet Mock Orange, relates to the similarity of the scent to that of orange blossom. *P. coronarius,* the earliest import to Europe, has been superseded by newer, better, larger-flowered varieties. It is, however, very reliable, floriferous and fragrant. It makes a round, spreading bush up to 3m high; the leaves are rather dull, being ovate, toothed and mid-green in colour. The double flowers, which appear in early summer, are not completely white; there is a dash of cream in them.

Some 40 species of this genus exist. Most are deciduous, although *P. mexicanus,* the Mexican Mock Orange, stays evergreen in mild climates. *P. coulteri,* the Rose Syringa, has petals that are stained purple-red, an effect also seen in the hybrid 'Belle Etoile'.

CULTIVATION

This plant is extremely easy to cultivate, and usually flowers very well even when thoroughly neglected. It does not really need to be pruned, although thinning out older wood after it has flowered is helpful to it. Apart from leaf spot, it is largely immune to pest and disease damage. It will grown in an ordinary (even dry) soil, well dressed with compost and lime in either sun or partial shade, although it flowers better in sun. Propagation is from hardwood cuttings taken in autumn.

FEATURES

Height: 3m
Flowering period: Early summer
Colour: White
Scent: Overpowering

1 Petal
2 Stigma
3 Stamen

1
2
3

PLATANUS ORIENTALIS

Oriental Plane Tree

*P*LATANUS ORIENTALIS is famous as much for the fact that it is a parent of The London Plane as for its own qualities. It is, however, a tree well worth growing. It has a long and distinguished documented history, and has been domesticated and planted since ancient times in Europe and northern India (Kashmir). It comes from Greece and other countries which border the Adriatic: Yugoslavia, Bulgaria and Albania. Hippocrates, the "Father of Medicine", taught his students under an Oriental Plane which, supposedly, can still be found on the island of Cos. He lived in the 5th century before Christ, so this story rather strains one's credulity. In Turkey there still exists a plane near which crusaders are supposed to have camped during the First Crusade. This tree has several stems which are fused together, a fact which foxed the French botanist Augustin Pyrame de Candolle, who estimated in the early 19th century that it was 2,000 years old. It is probably much younger than that.

The Oriental Plane was first brought to Britain at the end of the 16th century, probably from the Near East by an agent of the Levant Company. William Turner, in 1548, maintained that he knew two specimens of it in England, but it seems likely that he misidentified it (or was mistaken). Since then *P. orientalis* has been grown in many countries, doing particularly well in cities due to its toler- ance of atmospheric pollution.

P. orientalis differs from The London Plane in having a shorter and more rugged trunk and maple-like leaves which are more deeply lobed. It has a very large and handsome spreading crown of branches which makes it an excellent shade tree. Its bark is especially attractive, being mottled with silvery-grey and tan patches. The leaves are up to 23cm wide, with five or seven deep lobes and the fruits are balls, two to six of which hang on a long stalk after the leaves have fallen. The London Plane is a hybrid between *P. orientalis* and the Western Plane, *P. occidentalis.*

CULTIVATION

The Oriental Plane is very easy to grow; not only will it grow happily in any reasonable soil provided the position is not shaded, but it is tolerant of hard pruning if planted in too confined a space. Young trees should be fed with an annual slow-release fertilizer and receive sufficient summer watering. It can be propagated from hardwood cuttings in winter or soft tip cuttings in summer.

FEATURES

Height: Up to 30m
Flowering period: Throughout summer
Colour: Pale green

1 Pericarp
2 Seed coat
3 Endosperm

PLATYCODON GRANDIFLORUS

Balloon Flower; Chinese Bellflower

*T*HIS intriguing plant is closely related to the Campanula, and derives its common name from the shape of the flower-buds, which do resemble inflated balloons. It has always been much prized in its native northern China, Siberia and Japan for its medicinal properties. It first arrived in the West in 1782, but these days is not much grown. Far more common is the compacter variety of it which was sent home to Britain from Japan by Charles Maries. He was a professional collector sent out by the Veitch nursery in 1877, and he found *Platycodon grandiflorus* var. *mariesii* on the island of Yezo. The type species grows up to 60cm tall and has oval leaves and very pretty china-blue, saucer-shaped flowers in succession throughout summer.

CULTIVATION

Platycodons do not present many problems in cultivation, provided you take into account the fact that they are late to start into growth in the spring: it is all too easy to decapitate the new growths with a careless hoe, having quite forgotten that the plant was there at all. Otherwise, they are quite happy to remain undisturbed in a reasonably fertile and drained garden soil in a sunny place. Gertrude Jekyl grew both the usual type and the dwarf *P.g.* var. *mariesii* in her rock garden. They look especially good in open borders. In very hot districts they require semi-shade. Water regularly and feed with a complete fertilizer in spring.

Propagation is best done by seed for the roots do not like to be dug up and divided. Division should be done in winter, if at all. Seed is sown during autumn and will germinate in a fortnight at a temperature of 21°C. Seeds should not be covered. The little plants have to be handled very gently because of the incipient roots.

FEATURES

Height: 60cm
Flowering period: Summer
Colour: China blue

1 Petal
2 Stamen
3 Stigma
4 Sepal

PLUMERA ACUTIFOLIA
Frangipani

THIS small tree with its highly intoxicating scent first reached Europe from its native America — where the flowers were used by the Aztecs in religious rites and the sap by Amazonian Indians as an antidote for inflammation — in 1493, carted back by an Italian conquistadore, Count Mercuteo Frangipani. This act would seem to clinch the origin of *Plumeria acutifolia's* common name, frangipani, yet this is uncertain. Alternatives include an adaptation of the French *franchipanier* for coagulated milk — a reference to *Plumeria's* sticky white sap which flows easily whenever a branch is cut — or an Italian perfumer called Frangipani who concocted a scent for Catherine d'Medici from orris root, spices and musk that smelt remarkably like frangipani fragrance. Whatever the origin of the plant's common name the inspiration for its Latin tag is quite unmistakable, being named for Charles Plumier, a French priest and plant hunter whose *Nova Plantarum Americanarum Genera* (1703) detailed some 100 species, including frangipani, that he collected during several trips to the Americas in the late 17th century. Several varieties and hybrids and other species exist, including *P. obtusa,* an evergreen that boasts almost pure white blossoms grouped in clusters on a single stalk, and *P. rubra* which features red flowers. However, the two most common species are *P. acutifolia* and *P. fragrantissimum.*

The former is a common sight in many frost-free tropical or warm temperate Australian gardens, where it is usually grown as a shrub and, less frequently, a tree reaching 6.5m in height at maturity. During winter this deciduous tree assumes a rather grotesque profile, resembling a large candelabra, a shape that has inspired the name Dead Man's Fingers. Long leathery leaves appear at the tip of each branch during spring, followed by tight clusters of heavily-scented and waxy flowers, which litter the ground following summer rain storms. Due to hybridization the blossoms range in colour from cream through pink to red, but *P. acutifolia* has the classic colours of cream petals with yellow centres.

CULTIVATION

P. acutifolia can be grown in a pot from a sun-dried cutting in which the roots have developed — chop a branch off the parent tree and leave it lying in the sun to achieve this — and later transplanted in spring to a well-drained spot in fertile sandy soil. It flourishes in direct sunlight and is moderately resistant to salt conditions but needs protection from strong wind. Regular and thorough watering is necessary, and a complete fertilizer should be administered in spring. It is generally resistant to pests and diseases.

FEATURES

Height: 2m after 10 years to a maximum of 6.5m at maturity

Flowering period: Early summer to autumn

Colour: Cream petals with yellow centres

Scent: Strong

1 Style
2 Corolla
3 Stamens
4 Ovary

PRUNUS 'TAI-HAKU'

Great White Cherry

*P*RUNUS 'Tai-Haku', the Great White Cherry, is one of the 'Sato Zakura'; that is, the Japanese garden cherries. Like the others, it probably descends from the Hill Cherry, *Prunus serrulata* var. *spontanea,* but there may be other influences at work as well. It was grown in Japan for a long time, chiefly around Kyoto, but died out from there early in the 20th century. In 1923, Captain Collingwood Ingram, the great British authority on Japanese cherries (so much so that his nickname was "Cherry" Ingram) went to see a Mrs Freeman and her garden in Sussex. She told him how, in 1899 during a visit to Provence, she had met a Frenchman who had a Japanese friend prepared to send Japanese cherries to England. Mrs Freeman wrote to the Japanese friend and in the spring of 1900 received a small collection of cherries from him. Some of these plants had never been seen in England before. In Mrs Freeman's garden Ingram found one which he failed to recognize. It was almost dead, but he managed to propagate it from a few pieces of budwood, and discovered that this was 'Tai-Haku', a cherry which was by now extinct in Japan. Soon afterwards he had the satisfaction of reintroducing the plant to that country.

'Tai-Haku' is a very vigorous tree, and the flowers, which are large — up to 6cm across — are of the purest white and in spring made a stunning contrast to the leaves. These are bronze-red as they unfold, only later turning to green; in autumn they turn red and yellow before they fall. 'Tai-Haku' has distinctive bark with very big air-pores in it. This tree can grow to 9m high and spread a similar amount. It well deserves the title 'Great White Cherry'. Unfortunately it is difficult to find in Australasia.

CULTIVATION

'Tai-Haku' is not a difficult ornamental cherry to grow, provided its considerable spread is taken into account so that pruning is not necessary. The soil into which it is planted should not be too dry or, conversely, waterlogged; the soil nearby should not be deeply cultivated after planting, because the tree's roots tend to be shallow. The Japanese cherries are usually grafted plants and therefore not easy to increase. The best method is to bud the scion-wood onto a *P. avium* stock.

Cherries prefer cooler climates and rich soils. Aphids can be a nuisance, so spraying with Maldison is helpful. Ornamental cherries naturally suffer from the same diseases which afflict the fruit trees; for example bacterial canker, silver leaf and shot-hole. Attack by the first necessitates the cutting off of the cankered wood; attack by the last two requires at least the pruning of affected branches and often the grubbing up and burning of the whole tree.

FEATURES

Height: Up to 9m
Flowering period: Spring
Colour: White; young leaves bronze

1 Style
2 Petal
3 Stamen
4 Ovary

PUNICA GRANATUM

Pomegranate

*T*HIS plant has been the subject of many myths over the centuries, perhaps the most famous being that of the ill fated Persephone, who was condemned to spend four months a year in the Underworld because she ate half a pomegranate seed given to her by Hades.

Its Latin name is *Punica granatum;* the Romans called it *Malus punicum,* 'Apple of Carthage', because they obtained it from the area around Carthage, or *Malum granatum,* because of the grain-like seeds that the fruit contains. It receives a mention in the Bible, in *The Song of Solomon.* It originally came from Iran and Afghanistan, but is now grown all round the Mediterranean; it has been cultivated in Britain since the 16th century.

P. granatum is a deciduous shrub. The flowers are tubular with five to seven petals; the leaves are ovate or oblong and shiny. The fruit is a berry with a leathery skin and soft flesh which is formed by the outer seedcoats (arils) of the numerous seeds. The juice from the fruits can be used to make the drink Grenadine.

The most commonly grown pomegranate in Australia and New Zealand is called 'Wonderful' and it produces a purple fruit.

CULTIVATION

Pomegranates grow best in Mediterranean climates, i.e. those with long dry summers — ideal conditions for ripening the fruit. They do well in most soils but prefer a well-drained spot with full sun in deep, heavy soil that has been thoroughly composted beforehand. It may be necessary to water young plants until they are established, but once they reach maturity they are able to withstand drought conditions. They can be propagated either from seed or from hardwood cuttings. Seedlings produce fruit of varying quality but cuttings, taken in winter from reliable trees, are more likely to produce good fruit. Pomegranates can be grown either as shrubs up to about 3m or else as trees up to double that height. For trees, growth is encouraged by removing side shoots. Light pruning of outer growth will maintain the tree's shape. They are fairly resistant to pests and diseases, although fruit fly can be a problem in some regions.

FEATURES

Height: 3m
Flowering period: Summer
Colour: Scarlet; fruit a deep yellow, orange or purple

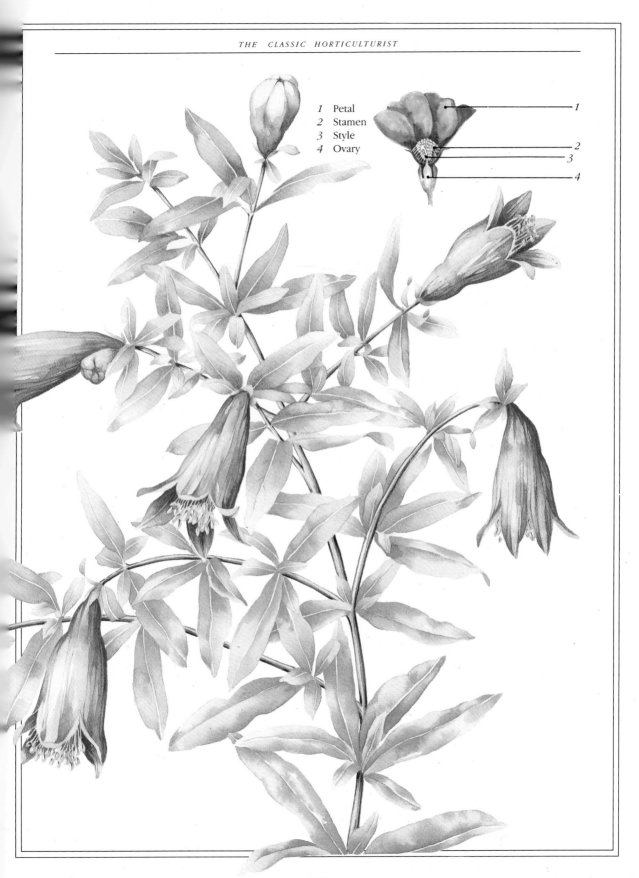

1 Petal
2 Stamen
3 Style
4 Ovary

RHODODENDRON ARBOREUM

The Tree Rhododendron

*R*HODODENDRON, meaning a rose tree, is the name given to this genus by Linnaeus in 1753. *R. arboreum* was the first Himalayan species to be collected and introduced to Europe. A red-flowered form was first found, by a Captain Thomas Hardwicke of the Indian Army in 1796: he found it flowering in Kumaon, southeast of Dehra Dun, in the Himalayas. However, this rhododendron is reputed not to have flowered in England until 1825, so Hardwicke's original must have been lost and a new introduction made at some time in the first few years of the 19th century. Either that, or the plant was not sent home at the time of discovery.

In a good situation this evergreen rhododendron can grow up to 6m or more. It has oblong-lanceolate and very leathery leaves (with a brown felt underside) up to 20cm long. The flowers, which are borne in dense trusses of about 20, normally bloom in spring. Besides the hybrids, there are also several forms of the species, including *R.a. cinnamomeum* (usually white-flowered and with cinnamon-coloured undersides to the leaves), which is the hardiest, and *R.a. campbelliae,* which has purple-pink flowers. Generally plants look best in a wilderness and informal garden.

The name is derived from the Greek — *rhodon* (rose) and *dendron* (tree). Over 800 species and many thousands of hybrids and varieties exist.

CULTIVATION

Rhododendrons in general like cool, moist, semi-shaded, sheltered conditions in enriched medium soil. They are intolerant of lime and demand perfect drainage. New Zealand and the temperate parts of Australia, preferably away from sea level, offer the best prospects for rhododendrons although they can be grown in subtropical regions, where adequate drainage is even more important because of heavier rain in summer. Plants will not grow well in soils that dry out and become hot during summer.

When planting it is important to loosen up the root system, which has a tendency to compact into a ball. If lifted from the ground they are best transplanted between late autumn and early spring but otherwise can be put in the ground at any time from pots. They must be planted no deeper than the soil surface in the container, and peat or leafmould can be put around the roots. Growth is improved by the application of a mixed fertilizer in spring. Pruning is unnecessary if the plants are well-shaped. Propagation is from semi-hardwood cuttings taken in late summer or by layering, which is the fastest way of producing a new plant, with most rhododendrons striking in six to twelve months. Rhododendrons are relatively free of disease although petal blight is common in warm areas, as is sun burn.

FEATURES

Height: 6m or more
Flowering period: Spring
Colour: Pink, red and white

1 Petal
2 Style
3 Stamen
4 Ovary

ROSA BANKSIAE BANKSIAE

Lady Banks' Rose

*R*OSES were among the earliest and most popular flower imports to Australia. Perhaps the first species to arrive was a wild climbing rose, *Rosa banksiae,* which was mentioned in the plant lists for Alexander Macleay's Elizabeth Bay House in the late 1840s. *R. banksaie* had been introduced to England from China by the Kew plant collector William Kerr in 1807 and named after the wife of his patron Sir Joseph Banks. The Banksia roses are ramblers that look best in semi-cultivated locations on the fringe of gardens, often acting as a bridge between formal arrangements and surrounding bushland. Their flowers are yellow or white, in single or double form. *R. banksiae banksiae* has masses of double white, violet-smelling blossoms, which grow in clusters along thornless branches, as described by the 20th-century English plant collector George Forrest during one of his forays into China:

> *I saw it in absolute perfection in the Lashipa Valley. Can you imagine a rose mass a hundred or more feet in length and twenty through, a veritable cascade of the purest white backed by the most delicate green with a cushion of fragrance on every side?*[20]

His colleague Reginald Farrer was similarly carried away, noting that *R. banksiae banksiae's* perfume had "an intoxicating sense of wine, and violets." It became a great favourite in 19th-century Australia, and specimens can still be found colonizing grave-yards and old gardens.

After falling from favour for many decades *R. banksiae banksiae* is now enjoying a revival. *R. banksiae lutea,* the Double Yellow Rose, which was introduced to England from China in 1827 and subsequently to Australia where it became extremely popular, has double yellow flowers.

CULTIVATION

R. banksiae banksiae is an extremely hardy plant, as its dogged survival in long-abandoned gardens proves. It thrives in Australia's warm temperatures and is able to survive dry conditions in a wide range of soils, ranging from sand to clay. However, it does best in fertile well-drained soil where it can receive plenty of sun. Regular and prolonged watering throughout spring and summer encourages the roots to go deeper, thus enabling the plant to better survive periods of dry weather. Planting is in mid-winter when *R. banksiae banksiae* is dormant. As roses are usually intended to grow for many years it is advisable to carefully prepare the ground with manure or compost, raising the bed to promote run-off. A slow-release fertilizer should be applied in spring. Because flowers are borne on old wood, trimming is best restricted to damaged wood or branches that are encroaching on pathways.

FEATURES

Height: 2m if trimmed as a shrub
Flowering period: Spring
Colour: White
Scent: Sweet

1   Stamens
2   Ovary
3   Petals

SALVIA PATENS

*L*ITTLE is known about the history of this plant except that it was introduced to the West from Mexico in 1838 and that seed was sent back on occasion by travellers who were interested amateurs attracted by the glorious colour of the flowers as well as by professional collectors. Robinson said that its brilliance was equalled by few flowers in cultivation. Gertrude Jekyll described its colour, along with that of Morning Glory and some of the gentians, as "perfectly pure blues. They are none too many and are, therefore, all the more precious in garden use." She used *Salvia patens* for summer border schemes, despite the fact that it was not hardy, by planting pot-grown plants in late spring. It is a perennial (in warm places) which grows no more than 76cm tall. The stem is hairy and, like all labiates, square in section. The leaves are oval and pointed, and the flowers, in colour the purest and deepest sky blue, are borne in summer. The genus includes some 500 species, including *S. splendens,* which has scarlet flower spikes; *S. officinalis,* which has blue flowers; and *S. horminum,* which has white, purple, blue, pink or red blooms.

CULTIVATION

The difficulty experienced by many gardeners in hanging onto this plant for long arises because of its tenderness. It will survive a mild winter in most districts, provided it is planted deeply and protected, but can fall victim to frosts and many people find it easier to treat it as a half-hardy annual and resow the seed each spring. Seed should be planted in moist soil when the temperature reaches 21°C and usually germinates within a fortnight. Alternatively propagation is by root division in spring and early summer. Salvias like a rich but light soil that is well drained and grow best in full sun. Growth is improved by enriching the soil with rotted compost or manure and by applying complete fertilizer in spring. Salvias need regular watering in dry weather, and they bloom profusely, making them ideal borderers, in summer.

FEATURES

Height: 76cm
Flowering period: Summer
Colour: Sky blue
Scent: Aromatic leaves

1 Stamen
2 Style
3 Petal
4 Sepal
5 Ovary

SCHIZOSTYLIS COCCINEA

Kaffir Lily; Crimson Flag

*S*CHIZOSTYLIS COCCINEA, known as the Kaffir Lily, comes, like so many good "bulbs", from South Africa. In autumn it bears up to twelve rich red star-shaped flowers in spikes on long — up to 90cm — stems above grassy, sword-shaped leaves. The unusual time of flowering, coupled with the innate charm of the flowers, makes this a highly desirable plant, and its variety 'Major' is worth seeking out for its larger flowers set on even sturdier stems. The most vigorous is 'Viscountess Byng'; this is pale pink and blooms late, in autumn. (Viscountess Byng herself is supposed to have been unable to grow this plant successfully in the dry soil of Essex, which must have been something of a disappointment to her.)

In 1920 an English nurseryman holidaying in the West of Ireland came across a schizostylis with clear pink flowers in the garden of a village doctor. He bought the entire clump for £50 and showed the plant the following year in London under the name of 'Mrs Blanche Hegarty', thus ensuring immortality for the doctor's wife.

CULTIVATION

Schizostylis are South African rhizomatous perennials but nevertheless require a moist soil which will not dry out in summer. That means planting them in late winter in a sunny place which is, however, damp (easier said than done) and mulching them in spring with peat or similar material. Watering in dry summers is a help, as is, in cold winters, protecting their roots in exposed places in winter with bracken or straw. *Schizostylis* can be grown as pot-plants in conservatories, being plunged out of doors for the summer, regularly fed to help flower-bud initiation, and brought inside once they start to flower. If the plant is happy in the garden and thrives, it will need dividing every three years, as the clumps can become very congested. This entails pulling the clumps apart in the early spring and replanting them in groups of about five shoots. The main enemy of *Schizostylis* is *Botrytis,* which can affect them in the autumn; spraying with a fungicide will help.

FEATURES

Height: 60cm
Flowering period: Autumn
Colour: Scarlet

1 Style
2 Petal
3 Stamen
4 Ovary

STRELITZIA REGINAE

Bird of Paradise

*T*HIS weirdly beautiful flower, resembling some strange prehistoric bird with its beak wide open, is a favourite with Australian gardeners. A native of South Africa, it was originally introduced to the outside world, where it became an immediate hit in gardening circles, by the great Scots botanist Francis Masson, the first plant hunter to be sent out overseas by the authorities at Kew. Masson made several journeys into the wild interior of Cape Province — then virtually unexplored by Europeans — in 1772-74 and 1786-95. During his first trip Masson explored Table Mountain before setting off with an ox-cart and Dutch guide for the interior, teaming up en route with an ex-pupil of the great Linnaeus, Carl Thunberg. The pair were eventually forced to turn back by hostile natives, but the plant samples that Masson took back to Kew, some 400 new species, helped thrust the Gardens into a position of eminence in the botany world which ensured its survival as one of the major plant institutions. A protége of Sir Joseph Banks, Masson also collected plants in the Canaries, Azores, Madeira, West Indies and North America, publishing several books, including the classic *Stapeliae Novae, or . . . new Species of that Genus discovered in the Interior Parts of Africa.*

Strelitzia reginae was named for George III's Queen Caroline, a princess from the House of Mecklenburg-Strelitz in Germany. An evergreen shrub, *S. reginae* is distinguished by its bizarre blooms, consisting of orange flowers with bright blue tongues encased by long green bracts. The flowers are borne atop long pulpy stems which grow in clumps from grey-green leaves. Along with *S. augusta,* which has white flowers and purple bracts, *S. reginae* is a favourite for flower arrangements.

CULTIVATION

S. reginae can be planted from a pot in light, friable soils at any time of the year and does best in full sunlight with protection from the wind. it contrasts favourably with bushy shrubs and is also suitable for rockeries and large tubs. The Bird of Paradise needs regular and thorough watering and should be fed with a complete fertilizer in spring. It is pruned by removing new suckers at the base of the clump.

FEATURES

Height: 1m at 10 years; 2m at maturity

Flowering period: Throughout the year

Colour: Orange and blue

1 Sepals
2 Petal
3 Ovary
4 Style
5 Stigma

SYRINGA PERSICA

Persian Lilac

S YRINGA PERSICA was brought to Europe, like the Common Lilac, thanks to the good offices of a diplomat — in this case the Venetian ambassador to Constantinople, who brought it back with him some time before 1614. It is supposed to have been introduced to Britain by John Tradescant the Elder about 1620, after he had volunteered to join the pinnace *Mercury* to fight against the corsairs of the Barbary Coast who were giving trouble to British shipping in the Mediterranean. That may or may not be true, but certainly by 1640 Parkinson was reporting that Tradescant was growing it at Lambeth. For a long time the plant was thought to be a jasmine — indeed, Hanmer referred to it as such in 1659. The word "syringa" comes from the Greek *syrinx,* meaning "panpipes", and alludes, as we have noted before, to the fact that the stems, if hollowed out, can be used to make musical pipes. By 1785, three forms were being grown: a blue one, a white one and a cut-leaved variety. About 1777, in the Botanic Gardens at Rouen, the ordinary Common Lilac, *S. vulgaris,* was crossed with it, the result being the hybrid called the Rouen lilac (*S.* × *chinensis*).

S. persica is a deciduous shrub, growing to no more than 2m high; it is,

therefore, more compact and less straggly than the Common Lilac. It is bushy and rounded, with lanceolate leaves that are green and up to 6cm long and 1cm wide. It has flowers which are pale lilac, and it is very scented. The dense panicles of four-petalled flowers come out in spring at the top of last year's growths. Shades of white, pink, purple, mauve, red-violet and primrose-yellow are also available.

CULTIVATION

Syringas do best in fertile alkaline soil where they receive at least half a day's sun. They also thrive on cold winters, and the roots should be kept as cool as possible. They are propagated from cuttings in summer or by ripened seed, although growth may be very slow if they are developed from seed. They need little pruning beyond dead-heading and the removal of dead and very weak wood at some point after flowering.

FEATURES

Height: 2m
Flowering period: Spring
Colour: Lilac
Scent: Very scented

1 Petal
2 Stamen
3 Style
4 Ovary

TULIPA CLUSIANA

The Lady Tulip

TULIPS were grown and developed in Turkish gardens by the 16th century and certainly caused excitement in the breast of Ogier Ghiselin de Busbecq, the Emperor Ferdinand's ambassador to Turkey. (He introduced *Philadelphus* to Europe at the same time — see page 126.) Unfortunately, de Busbecq misheard the name of this plant, thinking that the Turks called it *dulban,* which means "turban", when in fact they called it *lalé.* The mistake is odd because "tulip", for that matter, does not sound particularly like *dulban* either, and nor does the flower have more than a passing resemblance to a turban. Such considerations matter little; all that is important is that de Busbecq brought it to Europe in about 1554, and Clusius took bulbs to Holland with him when he became Professor of Botany at Leyden in 1593. (There is some doubt, however, that Clusius was the first to introduce the bulbs to Holland, a doubt reinforced by the fact that tulips had already arrived in England by 1578.) There is no space here to recount the tale of "Tulipomania", but we can note that fortunes were won (or, more often, lost) on this most dicey of gambles: the quality of the "breaks" on the flower of the new tulip. It was not until the 1920s that it was properly understood that the streaking on tulips, which made them so desirable and expensive, was the result of a highly capricious virus and ultimately harmful to the plant. By that time the whirlwind of "tulipomania" had long since blown itself out.

T. clusiana, like most of the other species tulips, comes from the hot regions of the eastern and northern Mediterranean — from Iran, Iraq and Afghanistan. It has solitary flowers which open out into a flat star-shape; these are white inside with a purple blotch in the centre, and white with red stripes on the outside of the petals. The flower is about 5cm in length, and each petal is pointed and something under 1.3cm wide. Its flowering period is spring. The leaves are very narrow, upright, and blue-green. The whole plant is no more than 15 to 30cm high. Yet, despite its diminutive size, it has a charm not vouchsafed to the larger, coarser garden hybrids. For one thing, the stiffness of the stem is not so obvious, and nor is the head out of proportion with the leaves and stem.

CULTIVATION

Tulips do best in more temperate climes, notably in New Zealand and south-east Australia, and prefer a rich, well-drained loam. Although generally sun lovers they will also thrive in partial shade. During dry spells before tulips flower they need to be watered thoroughly. The bulbs should be planted up to 15cm deep in autumn. Make sure the bulb is firmly positioned against the bottom of the hole; air pockets can collect water. The soil should be dressed with a complete bulb fertilizer. They look best if planted en masse. Lift the bulbs once the foliage has died down after flowering. The bulbs must be cleaned, sorted to size and stored in a dry, well-aired place until planting time. Although tulips are usually lifted annually *T. clusiana* can be left in the ground for several years if the soil is good and the bulbs healthy. Pests include aphids and, more seriously, *Botrytis.* Try spraying with benomyl, but if this fails to kill the virus the plants will have to be dug up and burnt.

FEATURES

Height: 15-30cm
Flowering period: Spring
Colour: White with red stripes on
the outside

1 Petal
2 Stigma
3 Stamen

VIBURNIUM TINUS

Laurustinus

*T*HIS is a shrub which has been cultivated in Britain for centuries, having been introduced from the Mediterranean region in the 1500s. It was called "Laurustinus" at that time because it was believed to be a kind of laurel, and the name has stuck. It has proved itself always a most useful shrub, not only because of its immense hardiness and its imperviousness to smoky atmospheres, but also because it is winter-flowering. It is not everyone's favourite, however. For example, the leaves smell unpleasantly; for E.A. Bowles, who was gifted with an extraordinary olfactory sensitivity, this plant was painful. He wrote of it that "in showery weather [they] exhale an odour of dirty dog-kennel and an ever dirtier dog".

V. tinus is an evergreen shrub which makes a dense, round shape, up to about 4m high in time. The branches come down to the ground, which makes it excellent for ground cover or alternatively as a hedging plant and screen. The leaves are glossy green and ovate, and have a prominent central vein. The small flowers, pink-tinged in bud and then white, are borne in terminal clusters throughout winter and into spring. The fruits are oval and pointed, and coloured the deepest blue. *V. tinus* 'Bewley's Variegated' has variegated flowers.

CULTIVATION

This is the viburnum most tolerant of ill-treatment. It thrives best in a sunny position and in good soil, but often it has to make do with less. If it is to give of its best, however, it should be planted in moist rich soil. It should be fed with a complete fertilizer in spring. It can be planted from a container at any time of the year. It does not require much pruning: a few very old and weak shoots can be cut out after flowering in May to promote growth and maintain shape. Propagation is from hardwood cuttings in winter and soft tip cuttings in summer. This plant can be layered. *V. tinus* has leathery, evergreen leaves which are not much attacked, except occasionally by thrips or red spider mite.

FEATURES

Height: Up to 4m
Flowering period: Late winter to spring
Colour: White
Scent: Unpleasant

1 Petal
2 Stamen
3 Stigma
4 Ovary

FOOTNOTES

1. HYAMS, E.   *A History of Gardens and Gardening* Dent, 1971

2. GUNTHER, R.T.   *Dioscrides De Materia Medica* Oxford University Press, 1921

3. HADFIELD, M   *A History of British Gardening* John Murray, 1960

4. FLEMING, L. & GORE, A.   *The English Garden* Michael Joseph, 1979

5. DESMOND, R.   *Dictionary of British & Irish Botanists & Horticulturists* Taylor & Francis, 1977

6. PARKINSON, J.   *Paradisi in Sole Paradisus Terrestris* Facsimile ed. Dover Publishing Inc, 1976

7. GUNTHER, R.T.   *Early British Botanists* Oxford University, 1922

8. WOODWARD, M.   (Ed.) *Gerard's Herbal (1636 Edition)* Gerald Howe, 1927

9. ALLEN, MEA   *The Tradescants* Michael Joseph, 1964

10. LEITH, ROSS, P.   *The John Tradescants, Gardeners to the Rose and Lily Queen* Peter Owen, 1984

11. DAWTREY, DREWITT   *The Romance of the Apothecaries Garden, Chelsea* Chapman Dodd, 1922

12. HAGBERG, KNUT   *Carl Linnaeus* Jonathan Cape, 1952

13. TAYLOR, GEOFFREY   *Some Nineteenth Century Gardeners* Skeffington, 1951

14. HOWE, BEA   *Lady with Green Fingers* Country Life, 1961

15. BUCHAN, URSULA   *An Anthology of Garden Writing* Croom Helm, 1986

16. MASSINGHAM, BETTY   *Miss Jekyll. Portrait of a Great Gardener* Country Life, 1966

17. JEKYLL, GERTRUDE   *Wood & Garden* Antique Collectors' Club, 1981

18. SCOTT JAMES, ANNE   *Sissinghurst, The Making of a Garden* Michael Joseph, 1975

19. PESCOTT, R.T.M.   *W.R. Guilfoyle, 1840-1912: The Master of Landscaping* Oxford University Press, 1974

20. McLEOD, J.A.   *Our Heritage of Wild Roses* Kangaroo Press, 1987

21. ANDERSON, A.W.   *The Coming of the Flowers* Norgate, 1950

SELECT BIBLIOGRAPHY

ALLEN, MEA   *Plants that Changed our Gardens* David and Charles, 1974

ANDERSON, A.W.   *The Coming of the Flowers* Williams and Norgate, 1950

BOWLES, E.A.   *My Garden in Spring* T.C.& E.C. Jack, 1914

BOWLES, E.A.   *A Handbook of Crocus and Colchicum for Gardeners* John Lane, The Bodley Head, 1952

BRAY, LYS DE   *Manual of Old-Fashioned Flowers* Oxford Illustrated Press, 1984

BRICKELL, C.D. & SHARMAN, F.   *The Vanishing Garden* John Murray, 1986

BRICKELL, C.D.   *Journal of the Royal Horticultural Society,* Volume 89, Part 1, January, 1964 (pp. 19-22)

Brunnings Australian Gardener Angus & Robinson, 1983

CAMERON, H.C.   *Sir Joseph Banks* Angus & Robinson, 1966

COATS, ALICE   *Flowers and their Histories* Hulton Press, 1956

COATS, ALICE   *Garden Shrubs and their Histories* Vista Books, 1963

COATS, ALICE   *The Quest for Plants* Studio Vista, 1969

CUFFLEY, P.   *Cottage Gardens in Australia* The Five Mile Press, 1983

FISHER, JOHN   *The Origins of Garden Plants* Constable, 1982

GENDERS, ROY   *The Cottage Garden* Pelham Books, 1983

GIBSON, MICHAEL   *Growing Roses* Croom Helm, 1984

GILBERT, L.   *The Royal Botanic Gardens, Sydney: A History 1816-1985* Oxford University Press, 1986

GORER, RICHARD   *The Growth of Gardens* Faber, 1978

GORER, RICHARD   *The Development of Garden Flowers* Eyre and Spottiswoode, 1970

HADFIELD, MILES   *A History of British Gardening* Murray, 1979

HYAMS, E. & McCQUITTY, W.   *Great Botanical Gardens of the World* Bloomsbury 1985

INGRAM, COLLINGWOOD   *Ornamental Cherries* Country Life, 1948

JEKYLL, GERTRUDE   *Wood and Garden* Antique Collectors' Club, 1981

JEKYLL, G. & WEAVER, L.   *Gardens for Small Country Houses* Antique Collectors' Club, 1981

KINGDON-WARD, FRANK   *Pilgrimage for Plants* Harrap, 1960

LEMMON, KENNETH   *The Golden Age of Plant Hunters* Phoenix, 1968

LOUDON, JANE   *The Ladies' Flower Garden of Ornamental Perennials,* 1844

LOUDON, JANE   *British Wild Flowers* Loudon, 1859

LOUDON, J.C.   *Encyclopaedia of Gardening (1822 edn.)* Loudon, 1822

LYTE, CHARLES   *The Plant Hunters* Orbis, 1983

LYTE, CHARLES   *Sir Joseph Banks* David and Charles, 1980

McLEOD, J.A.   *Our Heritage of Wild Roses* Kangaroo Press, 1987

MACAOBOY, S.   *What Flower is That?* Landsdowne Press, 1986

O'BRIAN, P.   *Joseph Banks: A Life* Collins Harvill, 1987

PATRICK, J.   *Gardens of Victoria* Australian Broadcasting Corporation, 1987

PESCOTT, R.T.M.   *The Royal Botanic Gardens, Melbourne: A History from 1845-1970* Oxford University Press, 1982

PESCOTT, R.T.M.   *W. R. Guilfoyle, 1840-1912: The Master of Landscaping* Oxford University Press, 1974

PLOWDEN, C. CHICHELEY   *A Manual of Plant Names* Allen and Unwin, 1970

PULTENEY, R.   *Botany in England* T. Cadell, 1790

READER'S DIGEST   *Illustrated Guide to Gardening* Reader's Digest, 1982

ROBINSON, WILLIAM   *The English Flower Garden* John Murray, 1898

ROYAL HORTICULTURAL SOCIETY   *The Dictionary of Gardening* (ed. Fred J. Chittenden and Patrick M. Synge) Oxford University Press, 1974

Royal Horticultural Society's Encyclopaedia of Practical Gardening Mitchell Beazley, 1980

SACKVILLE-WEST, V.   *V. Sackville-West's Garden Book* Michael Joseph, 1968

SALMON, J.T.   *New Zealand Flowers and Trees in Colour*

SEALE, A   *Allan Seale's Garden Companion to Bulbs and Perennials* Reed, 1985

STACKHOUSE, S.   *Shirley Stackhouse's Gardening Year* Angus & Robinson, 1981

SWANE, V.   *Valerie Swane's Australian Gardeners' Illustrated Catalogue* Angus & Robinson, 1983

TANNER, H.   *The Great Gardens of Australia* Macmillan, 1976

TAYLOR, JANE   *The Plantsman,* Volume 7, Part 3, December, 1985 (pp. 129-160)

TERGIT, GABRIELE   *Flowers through the Ages* Wolff, 1961

Yates Garden Guide for Australian Gardeners William Collins, 1987

SPECIALIST NURSERIES

ATHERSTONE GARDEN PLANTS (Old garden plants) Thomsons Road, Harcourt, Vic. 3453

BONNY' GARDEN CENTRE (Cottage flowers) 37 Parnall Street, Waroona, WA 6215

BROERSEN SEEDS AND BULBS (Flower seeds, bulbs and perennials) 365-367 Monbulk Road, Silvan, Vic. 3795

CHANDLERS NURSERY (Old-fashioned plants) 75 Queen Street, Sandy Bay, Hobart, Tas. 7005

DAVID THOMSON NURSERY (Rare plants, fuchsias) Gores Road, Summertown, SA 5154

DIGGER'S GARDEN CLUB (Flower seeds) 105 LaTrobe Parade, Dromana, Vic. 3936

HONEYSUCKLE COTTAGE (Cottage flowers, roses) Lot 35, Bowen Mountain Road, Bowen Mountain via Grosevale, NSW 2753

KENWICK ROSE GARDEN (Roses) 46 Osmond Street, Kenwick, WA 6107

KINGS HERB SEEDS (Flower and wildflower seeds) PO Box 14, Glenbrook, NSW 2773

KINGS HERBS (Flower and wildflower seeds) PO Box 19-084, Avondale, Auckland, New Zealand

NORGATE'S PLANT FARM (Hardy perennials) Blackwod Road, Trentham, Vic. 3458

ROSS ROSES (Old roses) St Andrews Terrace, Willunga, SA 5172

SPECIALITY SEEDS (Flower and British wildflower seeds) PO Box 34, Hawkesburn, Melbourne, Vic. 3142

SYDNEY WILDFLOWER NURSERY (Australian natives) Namba Road, Duffey's Forest, NSW 2084

TESSELAAR'S PADUA BULB NURSERIES (Bulbs, perennials and Californian wildflower seeds) Monbulk Road, Silvan, Vic. 3795

THE FRAGRANT GARDEN (Cottage flowers, English wildflower seeds) Portsmouth Road, Erina, NSW 2250

THE PERENNIAL COTTAGE GARDEN (Perennials) Hume Highway, Berrima, NSW 2577

TRELOAR ROSES (Old-fashioned roses and shrubs) Keillers Road, Portland, Vic. 3305

WOODBANK NURSERIES (Rare and unusual plants) Huon Highway, Longley, Tas. 7103

WOODSIDE HERBS (Rare and old-fashioned flowers, herbs) 100C Georges River Road, Kentlyn, via Campbelltown, NSW 2560

A SELECTION OF GARDENS OPEN TO THE PUBLIC

Although there are a few outstanding exceptions — Sydney's Botanic Gardens and Camden Park spring to mind — most of the earliest Australasian gardens of note date from the Victorian era and the majority are in New South Wales and Victoria. The following list, which contains public and private (which may not always be open) gardens, is definitive but serves as a good starting point for those interested in the history of gardening in The Antipodes.

ALTON, Mount Macedon, Vic. 3441

BEECHWOOD, Stirling, SA 5152

BOLOBEK, Mount Macedon, Vic. 3441

CAMDEN PARK, Nemagle, NSW 2560

CHRISTCHURCH BOTANIC GARDENS, Christchurch, New Zealand

CLARENDON, Evandale, Tas. 7212

CRUDEN FARM, Langwarrin, Vic. 3910

ERYLDENE, McIntosh Street, Gordon, NSW 2072

FLECKER BOTANIC GARDENS, Cairns, Qld. 4870

MAWALLOK, Via Beaufort, Vic. 3373

MILTON PARK, Hordens Road, Bowral, NSW 2576

NOOROO, Mount Wilson, NSW 2786

RIPPON LEA, 192 Hotham Street, Elsternwick, Vic. 3185

ROOKWOOD CEMETERY, Hawthorne Avenue, Homebush, NSW 2140

ROYAL BOTANIC GARDENS, Birdwood Avenue, South Yarra, Melbourne, Vic. 3141

ROYAL BOTANIC GARDENS, Mrs Macquarie's Road, Sydney 2000

VAUCLUSE HOUSE, Wentworth Avenue, Vaucluse, NSW 2030

WELLINGTON BOTANIC GARDENS, Wellington, New Zealand

OTHER USEFUL ADDRESSES

AUSTRALIAN COUNCIL OF NATIONAL TRUSTS, PO Box 1002, Civic Square, ACT 2608

AUSTRALIAN GARDEN HISTORY SOCIETY, PO Box 588, Bowral, NSW 2576

DIGGER'S CLUB, Digger's Garden Co. Pty Ltd, 119 Ashworth Street, Albert Park, Vic. 3206

GARDEN CUTTINGS, PO Box 279 Edgecliffe, NSW 2027

THE HERITAGE COUNCIL OF NSW, PO Box A284, Sydney South, NSW 2000

HERITAGE ROSES IN AUSTRALIA, C/- 5 Walker Street, Stirling, SA 5152

HISTORIC HOUSES TRUST, 61 Darghan Street, Glebe, NSW 2037

NATIONAL TRUST OF AUSTRALIA (NSW), GPO Box 518, Sydney, NSW 2000

NEW ZEALAND HISTORIC PLACES TRUST, Antrim House, 63 Boulchott Street, Wellington 1

INDEX

ACKNOWLEDGEMENTS

I should like to acknowledge gratefully the assistance of Dr. Brent Elliott and his staff at the Royal Horticultural Society's Lindley Library, and the staff of the University Library, Cambridge. I should also like to thank Toby Buchan for answering arcane queries so readily and my husband, Charles Wide, for his constant support.

URSULA BUCHAN

My grateful thanks to Dr. Brent Elliott and his assistant, Barbara Collecott, at the Royal Horticultural Society's Lindley Library for their invaluable assistance. I should also like to thank my wife, Rosamund, for her support, and apologise to my children for neglecting them during the preparation of this book.

NIGEL COLBORN

PICTURE CREDITS

p.9   By courtesy of the Trustees of the British Museum
p.10   Victoria and Albert Museum/E.T. Archive
p.11   Scala
p.12   E.T. Archive
p.13   National Gallery
p.14   Royal Horticultural Society/photo Eileen Tweedy
p.16   Bodleian Library
p.19   Victoria and Albert Museum/photo Eileen Tweedy
p.20   Victoria and Albert Museum/photo Eileen Tweedy
p.21   John Bethell
p.22   Ashmolean Museum
p.23   Royal Horticultural Society/photo Eileen Tweedy
p.24   Royal Horticultural Society/photo Eileen Tweedy
p.24   Hunt Institute for Botanical Documentation/ Carnegie Mellon University, Pittsburgh, Pa
p.25   Royal Horticultural Society/photo Eileen Tweedy
p.26   Royal Horticultural Society/photo Eileen Tweedy
p.26   Royal Society (portrait of Evelyn)
p.27   Royal Botanic Gardens, Kew
p.28   John Bethell

p.29   By courtesy of Her Majesty the Queen
p.30   E.T. Archive
p.32   E.T. Archive
p.33   E.T. Archive
p.34   E.T. Archive
p.35   Portrait of Sir Joseph Banks by Thomas Phillips, Dixson Gallery, State Library of New South Wales
p.35   The Dixson Gallery, State Library of New South Wales
p.36   Royal Horticultural Society/photo Eileen Tweedy
p.38   John Bethell
p.39   Royal Horticultural Society/photo Eileen Tweedy
p.40   Peter Herbert, Gravetye Manor
p.41   Peter Herbert, Gravetye Manor
p.42   Royal Institute of British Architects
p.43   Library of the Royal Botanic Gardens and National Herbarium of Victoria
p.44   Country Life
p.45   National Portrait Gallery
p.46   Sothebys
p.47   Edwin Smith
p.49   Royal Horticultural Society/photo Eileen Tweedy
p.51   John Bethell